BFI Film Classics

The BFI Film Classics is a [   ]s
and celebrates landmarks or world
argument for the film's 'classic' status, together with discussion of its
production and reception history, its place within a genre or national
cinema, an account of its technical and aesthetic importance, and in
many cases, the author's personal response to the film.

For a full list of titles available in the series, please visit our website:
<www.palgrave.com/bfi>

'Magnificently concentrated examples of flowing freeform critical poetry.'
Uncut

'A formidable body of work collectively generating some fascinating insights
into the evolution of cinema.'
Times Higher Education Supplement

'The series is a landmark in film criticism.'
Quarterly Review of Film and Video

'Possibly the most bountiful book series in the history of film criticism.'
Jonathan Rosenbaum, *Film Comment*

... nervously loquacious, at the edge of an abyss

Kenneth Burke

Marnie

Murray Pomerance

palgrave
macmillan

A BFI book published by Palgrave Macmillan

To Victor Perkins

First published in 2014 by
PALGRAVE MACMILLAN

on behalf of the

BRITISH FILM INSTITUTE
21 Stephen Street, London W1T 1LN
www.bfi.org.uk

There's more to discover about film and television through the BFI. Our world-renowned archive, cinemas, festivals, films, publications and learning resources are here to inspire you.

Palgrave Macmillan in the UK is an imprint of Macmillan Publishers Limited, registered in England, company number 785998, of Houndmills, Basingstoke, Hampshire RG21 6XS. Palgrave Macmillan in the US is a division of St Martin's Press LLC, 175 Fifth Avenue, New York, NY 10010. Palgrave Macmillan is the global academic imprint of the above companies and has companies and representatives throughout the world. Palgrave® and Macmillan® are registered trademarks in the United States, the United Kingdom, Europe and other countries.

Series cover design: Ashley Western
Series text design: ketchup/SE14
Images from *Marnie* (Alfred Hitchcock, 1964), © Geoffrey Stanley Inc.
The images on pp. 14, 21 (bottom), 24, 26–27, 32 (top two), 38–42, 48, 51–2, 59 (top), 76, 79 (top), 80 are from the collections of the Margaret Herrick Library, Academy of Motion Picture Arts and Sciences; the image on p. 59 (bottom) © Leo Fuchs

Set by Cambrian Typesetters, Camberley, Surrey
Printed in China

This book is printed on paper suitable for recycling and made from fully managed and sustained forest sources. Logging, pulping and manufacturing processes are expected to conform to the environmental regulations of the country of origin.

British Library Cataloguing-in-Publication Data
A catalogue record for this book is available from the British Library
A catalog record for this book is available from the Library of Congress

ISBN 978–1–84457–654–8

Contents

Acknowledgments

The author is grateful to: the late Jay Presson Allen, Bob Bowser, Jeanie Brown, Jenni Burnell, Jeffrey Byron, Monty Cox, C. O. 'Doc' Erickson, Alexandre Fuchs, Libbey C. Gagnon, Elliott Gould, Bill Krohn, Greg Landers, Dominic Lennard, Norman Lloyd, Lillian Michelson, Jenny Romero, Bill Rothman, Debbe Smith, Carol Tavris and Faye Thompson; and to Janet Lum, Associate Dean, Faculty of Arts, Ryerson University. This book has been made with the dedicated and gracious assistance of Sophia Contento, Philippa Hudson, Lucinda Knight and Jenna Steventon at BFI Publishing and Palgrave Macmillan.

The Story

Hiding behind a series of false identities, Marnie Edgar has been robbing Northern business establishments and repeatedly taking flight. She pays a visit to her mother in Baltimore, then secures a job at Rutland's, a Philadelphia publisher, where the scion of the family, Mark, falls in love with her. He entertains her at the races, brings her home to meet Dad. When she pilfers the company safe, he trails and catches her, angry and exasperated, then offers the choice of himself or the police. They marry. But on the honeymoon voyage Marnie is unable to consummate the union, confessing that she cannot bear to be touched by men. Back home at his family estate, after a gruelling fox hunt in which she misses a jump on her beloved horse and must destroy him, Marnie is completely withdrawn, hopeless, lost. Mark takes her to her mother's house where in a flashback remembrance, during a thunderstorm, she reconstructs a long-buried moment of horror and agony from her childhood. Released finally from the bonds of blocked memory, Marnie goes off with Mark toward a more open future.

1 Fugue

Marnie Edgar is on the run. Our first glimpse finds her already in
motion, striding confidently away from the camera on an empty
railway platform, modernity apotheosised, her body fitted snugly
into tweeds, her styled hair black as coal. Beneath her arm is a fat
purse, a labial pouch in Provocation Yellow. We glide behind (the
purse gripping our gaze), she stops to wait, and the scene fades.
Soon later,[1] two suitcases are open on a nondescript hotel bed, the
silks of a soiled identity tossed into one, a crisp new masquerade
folded into the other. A sheaf of ID cards hides behind the mirror of
her compact. In the bathroom, a head plunged into the sink … that
black industrial identity rinsed down the drain … and arising into
camera view, brilliantly doubled in the mirror, the platinum hair of –
    Our girl, eyes bright with triumph, complexion alabastrine.
She has escaped, whatever the trap: in this case the bloated, piggy face
of Strutt (Martin Gabel), grunting everlasting possession – 'Robbed!'
– insatiable jealousy, resentment, malicious hunger for revenge.
    In the explosion of that proud, beautiful face inside the wet ring
of sparkling hair, we already loved her.

In dreams awake

Alfred Hitchcock proclaimed the chase 'the final expression of the
motion picture medium', adding that its tempo and complexity were
'an accurate reflection of the intensity of the relations between the
characters' (pp. 125, 129). Arriving in Philadelphia,[2] Marnie ('Tippi'
Hedren) neatly deposits her old suitcase into a 30th St Station locker,
the key into a heating grate on the floor.[3] At Rutland & Co., under
the pseudonym 'Mary Taylor', she applies earnestly for a job.
The young boss, Mark (Sean Connery), is watching with interest; he
gives the nod. Training with ever diligent Susan Clabon (Mariette

Hartley[4]), then calmly scouting the premises of the office manager Ward (S. John Launer[5]) – in order that Marnie would stand out in it, specific instruction was given that Ward's office should be painted a pale colour (Robertson to Boyle) – she makes plans to fleece her new employer. A habitual thief (and, as she presents herself here, widow), and trailing a chain of previous robberies and sloughed identities wherever she goes, Marnie springs directly from Winston Graham's 1971 novel, which had been agented to Hitchcock's assistant Peggy Robertson (Hall, *Robertson*: p. 231). Hitchcock's practice was to treat popular fiction as Marnie treats employment, extract the principal treasure without obligation – to the author's style, overall theme, or plot.[6] If ever he had a female alter ego (as implied by Maxwell Coplan's strange photograph in François Truffaut's important interview book [p. 321]) Marnie is her epitome.

In the washroom late one afternoon, she secretes herself in a stall until all the other employees have gone home (on Hitchcock's obsession

Stalled; on tiptoe

about toilets, see Spoto: p. 415 and note). Then, 'borrowing' the safe combination from its hiding place inside Susan's desk (forgetful Ward must consult it several times a day), she nabs the company funds and tiptoes off, past the cleaner (Edith Evanson), who would hear Marnie's shoe drop if she weren't deaf. Flight is the theme: from her recent past; from her complicating job at Rutland's; from the fact of her thievery (she proclaims herself an innocent); and then, upon her beloved stallion Forio, from every binding divot of turf which might position her in a fully drawn present. Only in the finale (which I will address at the finale of this book) do we learn how all of Marnie's flights compose a single whirlwind escape – from a long-lost yesterday. In film, every moment is a flight from the moments before.

Unreal

Stalwart, sleek, and gleamy black, Forio is the one constant and true repository of love in Marnie's life. She would fain visit her mother in Baltimore, but first a digression to Garrod's farm for a ride on Forio.[7] When Marnie is upon him a different kind of flight is involved, something more akin to the fugue states discussed in psychoanalytic theory, where locomotion is linked to neurosis. We have two senses of Marnie's fall from reality: her tight interconnection with, and cherishing of, Forio, thus divorce from the walkaday world through postural elevation and dependence upon the organic motion of another being (sex can, yet need not, be implied); and her race into the future at a speed no human body can achieve on its own. Because of the way Hitchcock shows her, she is separated, withdrawn into a private world split psychologically and cinematically from everyday space and time. Effects were not needed to cover Hedren: she could ride well – the shot of her trotting toward the camera on Forio, and discovering the stoically angry figure of Mark, is made without a stand-in, in one fluid take ending on a close-up of 'Tippi' in the saddle. Yet most of the horseback shots were done in studio against a rear-projected background, thus depositing a strange dislocation and oneiricism in which Marnie floats, even flies, with the green world

dropping away as in another dimension. More daydream than reality, these shots are invested with considerable affect and bear 'traces of both the occasion which engendered [them] and of some past memory' (Freud: pp. 45, 48). In the close-ups, a beatific remove is etched on her features as she bathes in an eery light.

While the argument could be made (by anyone unfamiliar with the technicalities of rear-projection filming) that Hitchcock is an unprofessional failure here – even his assistant thought 'it didn't look good' (Hall, *Robertson*: p. 284) – we should recall his attraction to process work and cinematographer Robert Burks's origins in special effects. Hitchcock knew how to get what he wanted, and how to vary the rear-projection effect. Later in the film, for instance, we see rear projections that are entirely imperceptible as such (for example, at the racetrack). Hitchcock intended Marnie's riding sequences to appear precisely as they do: intermediates between unaffected reality and artful construction. They permitted him to lure his audience in two contradictory directions at once, away from and toward total identification with Marnie, who wants frantically to be only where she is. On Forio she can flee from a mother (Louise Latham), who, over-steeped in upright Christian values, apparently loathes her own daughter. Forio is the vehicle of Marnie's soul, uplifting and redeeming her.

A similarly stunning separation or fugue occurs in the tiny Baltimore street where Bernice Edgar lives – 'just like the north of England' (Hitchcock to Hunter). Marnie is making another of her seemingly routine, if infrequent, visits early in the film, bearing a fur stole (spoils of the Strutt conquest but attributed to a beneficent, entirely fictional 'Mr Pemberton', for whom she 'works'). Much later, she is dragged back there when Mark, having discovered that Marnie's mother is not 'dead', and working out the moral obligations of his sincere love to the last turn, insists on solving the dark puzzle that has locked the young woman into herself. Both scenes include long and medium shots of the street, with children singing the strange little skipping rhyme 'Mother, Mother, I am ill/Call for the doctor over the hill'.[8] Hitchcock had wanted here to replicate a street running off London's East India Dock Road: 'You turn the corner and suddenly, there's a ship! It's in the street. You know, it's actually at the end of the road' (Albert Whitlock quoted in Krohn, *The Birds*: p. 41). His designer Robert Boyle worked with scenic artist Harold Michelson to make a huge backdrop with a ship painted on it, and Burks shot the scene to simulate first a sunny, then a rainy, day. Technically speaking, the 'reality' is distorted:

He wanted this looming image. And you know what it was. We tried to dissuade him and that's where we made a mistake. He dug his heels in and he was determined to get this damned image, which, of course, was no longer possible, because really all we would see in 1.85[9] would be the hull. What would that mean? It would be just a black ... totally unreadable. Harold had to keep drawing it so that the superstructure came in, so that you could see the funnel ... and now it's a ship and now it's also too damn small. (Whitlock quoted in Krohn, *The Birds*: p. 41)

Many viewers detect a difference in realisation between this background and the brick row-houses, so that, expecting in movies only radical extremes of 'realism' or 'artifice', they judge Hitchcock's vision sloppy, amateurish, and out of key.[10] But the vision is perfectly achieved, since some intermediate state of mind between being at rest in her dream world of freedom and finding herself trapped in the socially determined and morally strict confines of Bernice's home now afflicts, disturbs, displaces, even torments Marnie. Further, the performance rhythm and diegetic continuity would be interrupted, ruinously exaggerated, were Hedren to fully *enact* the emotional panic and distanciation Marnie feels. Her feelings are projected outward by way of the lighting and scenery, the qualitative

Stage 21 at Universal set for filming the finale at Bernice's house (11 February 1964)

distinctions that find their way to the eye. Marnie always feels one thing and does another, and the technique of doubling the screen actually mounts her doubled being as a visual concern.

Marky Mark

From Mark Rutland, too, Marnie is in flight. As a person, as a male, and as a capitalist, he antagonises her. The film is a map and history of this *agon*. Superficially an icon of the managerial class, scion of the Rutland publishing fortune – the 1960s antedated the digital revolution – Mark is a 'marker' of *the* staple transactional, economic *materiél* of Western culture. 'The oral tradition [of the Greeks] emphasized memory and training,' writes Harold Adams Innis, but 'we have no history of conversation or of the oral tradition except as they are revealed darkly through the written or the printed word' (p. 9). By the sixteenth century, 'an enormous increase in production and variety of books' and, by 1800, 'the invention of the paper machine and the introduction of the mechanical press involved a revolution in the extension of communication facilities' (p. 27). Money, legal texts, literature, advertising: by 1950 all of these were handled through publication.[11] Marnie has placed herself in conflict with dominant peers of the economic system, having undertaken as a hobby (now become quasi-professional) what sociologists call 'craft thievery':

Criminal craftsmen have always had to adopt some way of relating to the police to minimize their effectiveness. The simplest and most obvious way of relating is avoidance, and, as we have seen, many of the techniques of craft crime serve to prevent people, including the police, from knowing a crime is taking place and, when they have found out, from knowing who did it. ... Trying to evade police notice can take up a great deal of time and energy and, if the police are at all effective, is not invariably successful. (McIntosh: pp. 114–15)

The precise focus of Marnie's resentment and stylised aggression is the private property for which Mark and his business enterprises stand. She has opted for a path that leads away from his. Yet he is in love with her.

One rainy Saturday afternoon, the new employee has come in to type the boss's manuscript, *Arboreal Predators of the Brazilian Rain Forest*. Near his desk, in an ornate frame, is a lovely colour photograph of Sophie the jaguarundi, whom Mark taught to trust him. A thunderclap and lightning flash terrify Marnie, and a tree branch crashing through the window shatters a cabinet of pre-Columbian artifacts – all Mark had that belonged to his deceased wife. The 'rain forest' is thus both outside the frame and inside this room; and Marnie, her eyes as fearfully alert as Sophie's, is become an arboreal predator herself. In this tight little scene we discover Mark's deeper passions, his articulate and gentle manner, his authorial status, his education, his voyaging experience, and his social class (genuine pre-Columbian figurines are priceless). The lightning makes Marnie see red. As we saw at her mother's

Sophie

house, when she froze in terror before a bouquet of red gladioli, something about this colour touches a nerve so deep she has no access to its root, no retrievable memory, nor any reserves for handling her fear in everyday situations. Mark draws her into his arms, leans into her face. A tender kiss, but also, Hitchcock emphasises, a fugal one: while the lips approach and touch, we glide in for not only a close-up but an extraordinary macro-close-up (rare in his oeuvre) and there is a slight slow-motion effect. The mouths are beastly, and the scene ends soon afterward.[12]

Yet the kiss leaves Marnie, if to some degree physically pleased, wary and on edge. Very like Sophie prior to Mark's care, she is in flight from trust.

A design

Mark drives Marnie to meet his father at Wykwyn, the family's farm-estate, where the old man (Alan Napier) reposes in a contented aura of retirement accompanied by Lil Mainwaring (Diane Baker), Mark's sister-in-law (and a young woman whose hunger for him could hardly be more palpable). Marnie makes a hit with Dad, and the couple are soon – too soon, thinks Lil – engaged. Hitchcock's *mise en scène* of the post-connubial departure and South Seas honeymoon artfully displays Marnie's sullen, obedient, even formalist acquiescence to, and adept performance of, the choreography of courtship and wedlock. There is never a giveaway love twinkle in her eyes, but her manners cannot be faulted. Mark, however, is honestly hungry for love, with Marnie – stiff, withdrawn, and physically remote – undeniably reluctant to feed him. Her seemingly 'frigid' flight (as female failures at heterosexual generosity were often called in the 1960s) from Mark's notably itchy desire comes to a head at sea. She is stand-offish to a fault, night after night deflecting his reserved and dignified patience. Can she possibly keep up the dodge until he wearies of trying?

Shipboard at dinner, Mark suddenly offers a little anecdote meant to be friendly and therapeutic, but somewhat ambiguous, about Marnie's condition:

In Africa, in Kenya, there's quite a beautiful flower. It's coral-coloured with little green-tipped blossoms, rather like a hyacinth. Now, if you reach out to touch it, you discover that the flower was not a flower at all, but a design made up of hundreds of tiny insects called fattid bugs. They escape the eyes of hungry birds by living and dying in the shape of a flower.

'Such protective imitations exist widely in nature', wrote Robert Ardrey, whose conversation with R. S. B. Leakey may have inspired Jay Presson Allen's scripting of this tale (p. 67). Ostensibly an illustration of his zoophilia (yet featuring an incorrect articulation of the name of the flatid [or flattid] bug), Mark's tale diagnoses Marnie's emotional withdrawal as a self-protective tactic, as though, surrounded by predators, she has built a defensive barrier. But for a man in Mark's social position the 'predator' is the deviant type, the criminal who would penetrate his fortress to steal his wealth: in short, Marnie herself. For Marnie, the threat is any official hunter out to catch wild things such as she: the police on her tail, harsh Strutt or his coeval, Mark. While it is true that she does cover herself with designs to keep off the 'hounds', Marnie's troubles extend to sexual 'hunters' as well; predation is her only assured means of survival. From her point of view (as an experienced observer), the decoration of the 'fattid' bug relates more directly to social displays put on by those who would cover their greed and lust, people who never say what they mean and almost never mean what they say. All through the film, Marnie flees from believing Mark when he says he loves her.

Clean

Occasions repeatedly present themselves for Marnie to escape from spaces of normative heterosocial relations to lavatories where, her social presence closeted, she descends to a more unitary, introspective, private experience. Bizarrely for a popular heroine, Marnie retreats to the bathroom four times through the narrative – and the camera with her, so that her 'flight' is clearly accessible (see also Pomerance, *Eye*: pp. 141–50). It is in a bathroom that we saw

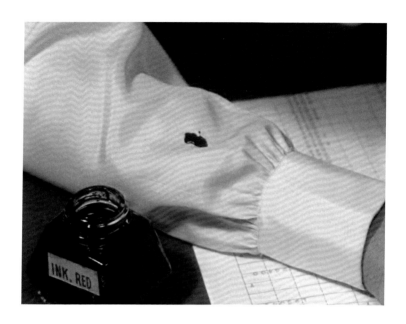

her transformation at the beginning of the film, as the running water (a continual flow, like the incessant unspooling of film) transmogrified the black hair into blonde and in the telltale mirror the new identity was revealed.[13]

Next: early on at Rutland's, Artie the office boy (Linden Chiles) flusters Marnie with his attentions, so that upon her pristine white blouse she spills a staining blot of red accountant's ink. 'THE SCENE IS ONCE AGAIN SUFFUSED WITH A RED GLOW' reads the shooting script (29 October 1963). Seeing red in such high contrast,[14] she flips into neurotic panic (as when she saw the red flowers and the red lightning) and flees to the washroom for cleansing. The stain is many things at once, not least a trigger for her fugue: a *macula* indicating sin and expiation as signal forces; a smear of blood, pointing to Marnie's presumptive 'virginal' status; an indicator of numbers, profits and losses, and thus a signpost to the safe she intends to rob; and an exemplary case of what Slavoj Žižek has called

The blot

'the Hitchcockian blot', a figure or arrangement that confounds and later unravels a narrative.

A third scene prefaces the Rutland's robbery, as Marnie waits in a toilet stall while the other secretaries wash up, chat enthusiastically, and drift away. Who but Hitchcock, arranging for theft, would set up the scene here? 'The image of Marnie, leaning against the wall and listening, is held for much longer than might seem justified by its apparent content. But that is just the point,' writes Victor Perkins. 'Once we have seen that Marnie is waiting and listening, there is nothing more for us to look at. Instead we do what she does. We wait. We listen' (p. 142). On the fourth washroom visit we are kept outside, with Mark, counting the minutes (forty-seven, claims he) while she 'prepares' herself for bed on the honeymoon cruise. Mark makes an elegant, if comically pompous, little speech:

The battleground of marriage is not, contrary to the movies and *The Ladies' Home Journal* ... I repeat, is *not* the bedroom. The real field of battle is the *bath*. It is in the bath and for the bath that the lines are drawn and no quarter given. Now it seems to me that we are getting off to a dangerously poor start, darling.

He (and Hitchcock through him) is centralising Marnie's body, a focus of concern and organisation, a 'battleground' that in the bath is groomed, sanitised, refreshed, made up, rehearsed, and exercised for deployment. We will come later to a shocking understanding of that body and its horrible meaning in this film.

Flight from self

The film never more pointedly reports on Marnie's ongoing flight from herself than when, first visiting Bernice, she finds at the door a polished little doppelgänger, cold, suspicious, with long gleaming blonde hair and suspecting eyes. This creature, Jessie Cotton (Kimberly Beck), seems to have occupied (roosted in) Marnie's position in the home. Marnie retracts, as though Jessie were living poison. Bernice even notices this and chides Marnie for her manner.

(top) Jessie Cotton answering the Edgar door; (bottom) Hitchcock working with Kimberly Beck

Soon later, Marnie lies abed in the shadows of her old room, thrown into terror by the recurrent sound of knocking in her nightmare. Her inner world is a mosaic of *cauchemars*, her waking life a constant navigation away from her past and inner self.

But another flight from self is more visible and subtler in *Marnie*. Marnie's arrogant brittleness of manner and hauteur of pose lift her above the world from which she pilfers. In order to see the evasiveness in her porcelain surface, it is necessary to divine in Hedren's brilliant performance a second expressive register, a skin beneath the skin, where she is vulnerably childlike (a second Jessie), not canny; sensitive and awkward, not calm and cool; wary and agonised, not prettily self-confident. The mature doll she plays (with the harsh, strident, critical voice) is but a vehicle for flight from the little beast she deeply is. Because she is so frightened and so helpless in a world filled with hungry hunters, Mark's reaching out to her can be seen as an act of the purest love. In sticking with Marnie he is 'betraying the team', that secretive pack of smart, aggressive men who run her world and whose touch Marnie cannot tolerate. Mark surrenders the flag of masculinist, corporate savvy to assist a person whom capitalist logic would simply abandon.

This dynamic between concern and trepidation is palpable onscreen: the gentle focus of Mark's eyes, the way Marnie shies from his face, the way her eyes seek inwardly for tactics and turns, the endurance of his smiling patience. He must be firm with her, yet he knows that firmness can be felt and read as torture. A negative view of Mark would see him at best as a tamer, whose ultimate goal is possession. But his voice with Marnie – it is in part for the resonance and lacquer of that voice that Connery was cast[15] – reassures us that only kindness is in play.

But at film's end – the film's very end: the new prelude after all these fugues – it becomes clear that even from kindness Marnie might run.

2 *Droit du Seigneur*

That honeymoon of Mark and Marnie's: let us invade it.

Having married him not so willingly – she may like Mark and trust him a little; but the alternative was entirely unappealing – Marnie has been escorted to a sleek ship that will sail the South Seas. Hitchcock boldly cuts from Wykwyn to the cabin interior, skipping the transitional steps in what became a lesson to his writer, who recalled apprehending 'more about screenwriting ... than I learned in all the rest of my career':

I only knew how to write absolutely linear scenes. So I wrote the wedding and the reception and leaving the reception and going to the boat and getting on the boat and the boat leaving ... I mean, you know, I kept plodding, plodding, plodding. Hitch said, 'Why don't we cut some of that out, Jay? Why don't we shoot the church and hear the bells ring and see them begin to leave the church. Then why don't we cut to a large vase of flowers, and there is a note pinned to the flowers that says, "Congratulations." And the water in the vase is sloshing, sloshing, sloshing.' Lovely shorthand. (Quoted in Auiler: p. 218)[16]

A luxury suite decorated in browns and beiges, set with vases of white and yellow chrysanthemums and pink gladioli, bolstered in comfortable green sofas. The privacy is virtually embarrassing, as by now we have empathised fully with Marnie's desperation to avoid intimate cloisters with this handsome, eager, but unfathoming man. She is now unprotected: at work she had the company of Susan and others; even in Mark's office-temple there were spirits: Sophie, the dead wife. At Garrod's she eloped with Forio in the wild openness of the green fields ('Whenever I was in a spot I thought of him' [Graham: p. 141]). Here, however, is the cramp of cabin comfort, with the silent sea waiting outside the porthole.

Shooting Mark and Marnie returning to Garrod's

Remembering a film is not the same as watching it. One passes back and forth through its corridors, gathering snatches out of syntactical order. Mark picked up Marnie/Mrs Taylor at Garrod's, waiting in the field with an irritated scowl for this thief, as he now knows her, to swing up to him on Forio. His tone was entirely snide, a little wounded: you can walk, I will ride. Back at the Red Fox, she offers as life story an elaborate lie (her mother dead; ditto a Mrs Taylor, the mother's former companion, from whom she inherited money and a house that she sold for $9,000). She is petulant, bratty, her long silences serving for the concoction of new lies. Driving back to Philadelphia (where to protect her reputation Mark figured his company's loss and replaced the money in Ward's safe), Mark admits recognising her from Strutt's (Strutt and Co. are the Rutland accountants). Big shock. She hated Strutt. 'The way you hate everybody?' A velveteen voice: 'Oh no, not you.'

One could follow the twists and turns of this meandering conversation, its evasions, its pursuits, Marnie's dead-end inventions, Mark's doubting third-degree – the form will be duplicated later as a fox hunt – but no matter what these combatants say, two extra-dialogic effects are salient. Throughout the duet, one hears Mark's assured, self-mocking, persistently graceful baritone, while Marnie is on edge, panicky, trapped, looking in every direction for an exit. Also, the rear projections behind Mark driving and Marnie riding are technically unmatched: the countryside passes more swiftly behind her, as though to emphasise the press of the rushing future (see Pomerance, *Eyes Have It*: p. 96). During a brief coffee stop at Howard Johnson's,[17] Mark will not let her out of his sight. And, purrs he, she need stick around for only a week, *until the marriage can be accomplished*. 'You're taking possession!' says Marnie in shock and he, with a Cheshire Cat smile, agrees: she needn't pilfer the Wykwyn silver, because soon enough it will be all hers.

After the ceremony Mark and Marnie are swiftly gone, but Lil and 'banking cousin' Bob (Bob Sweeney) linger in the doorway discussing the $42,000 ring, the $7,000 Mark insisted Bob cash for

him at the club one night, and the cost of the honeymoon cruise. '$70,000 in one week!'[18] Naughty Lil, her suspicions roused, sneaks into Mark's empty room and riffles through his chequebook. A note: 'Pay off Strutt.' And now to the cruise ship.

Words, words, words

'BON VOYAGE, BON VOYAGE, BON VOYAGE' in the lush bouquets. 'Would you like some bourbon to brush your teeth?' he asks chummily, but she is incommunicado in the bath, hence that little lecture – 'The real field of battle is the *bath*' – delivered quite as though to a note-taking audience, with all the proper pauses. He paces the

Connery and Hedren in the car mock-up for process photography

(top) From left: Bob Sweeney, Diane Baker, Sean Connery, 'Tippi' Hedren, Alan Napier and John Hart; (bottom) Hitchcock setting up the wedding tableau

stateroom, drink in hand, then sits on the bed, that dull altar outside the sacred laboratory where Marnie is at work. The door opens. She emerges. A pale sea-blue Pierrot robe, her blonde hair in bouffant, her cheeks scrubbed. 'You're very sexy with your face clean.'

Which face? The front of her head, which is only her humanity, or the personality she has chosen for 'keeping up' appearances? And what, after all, does it mean to *tell* someone she looks sexy, except to offer another (briefer) lecture? Words in profusion. Consider that we have already weathered a very long conversation: in Mark's office, at the track, at Wykwyn, in the car, at Howard Johnson's, in the car again, now here at sea. He has been chasing; she has been ducking away. At last he tries a kiss but this move beyond the precinct of language is 'fatal', provoking her to leap up, race across the room, and bury herself rigidly in a corner of the sofa, her pallid robe settling into the dark green cushions. She cannot bear to be touched. 'By me?' 'By anybody. Men.'

Cannot bear to be touched by men.

'I'll kill myself if you touch me!!!'

They will have to be kind to one another, says he.

'Kind!'

All right, then, he will be kind. She will be polite. And he swears on his honour that he will not— A pregnant vacuum as she gazes at her Knight.

There is more conversation – always more. She needs help, certainly, thinks he, perhaps a psychiatrist. Swiftly her feminism perks up: the moment a man doesn't get what he wants, 'Bingo, you're a candidate for the funny farm!' And what makes him think she needs help? (Such a very long conversation!) He paces, a load of frustration jammed into his posture. More than being bottled up sexually, he is confused by the patterns she flings out. He is an ethical man, bound to aid and improve her if he can, but also moral, laced into a corset of propriety and expecting the same of others, and here in the garden of marriage he is denied the fruits of the tree. She, who wants only to fight, is become his demon.

So very many words: she is from the South, has no husband, never had a husband or a beau 'or a gentleman caller';[19] that fear of being touched, him swearing on his honour not to—. Not to what? – the missing verb. Not to throw himself upon her like a *seigneur*? Through this labyrinth, the field at Garrod's, the inn, the car, the coffee shop, the wedding, the stateroom, her mounting terror that he will demand fulfilment and his mounting desire met by her evasions, the talk, the talk, the talk has reached the point of detonation ... yet still they jabber. Talk, a flight from action (just as talk about talk is a flight from a flight). Around and around the room (a nursery game), posing among the flowers, Mark with the promising pinks, Marnie with the dying golds.

Language serves mainly orientational ends. In this long sequence of scenes, the extent of the talk suggests that a great thrust of orientation is required. Why, with lust a-building, must Mark pronounce before making a play? Why, too, if Marnie smells his game,

'Kind!'

does she dodge before flatly turning off? By the time of the honeymoon, as Marnie shies from him onto that couch, Mark (formerly beneath us on what Thomas Scheff calls the 'ladder of awareness') has finally come to share our knowledge. He has walked into a cage. That he had eyes for Marnie and wanted to bed her, that his proprieties required marriage first are no claims to innocence and won't help.

The extensive dialogue constitutes Hitchcockian foreplay, alighting upon, tickling, then massaging viewers' expectation and voyeuristic hunger (the hunger an audience always feels, he knows). Hitchcock's catering to spectatorial appetite is doubly evident. First, Mark's dialogue articulately oozes breathy, pedantic self-consciousness, Connery using his polished voice and light burr to stretch or accent syllables, sound vocal embellishments, and generally *spell out* our concentration, pull and stretch our attentiveness like taffy. This is decorous beating around the bush. For her part, Hedren produces a synchronised alternation of stubborn rejection (infused with taciturn sullenness) and eyelash-batting seduction, plainly and simply teasing just as he is teasing her, and finally raising her voice into razor-sharp stridency.

To give a sense of the clock ticking (this honeymoon must seem to wear on without a thaw), Hitchcock introduces something uncharacteristic for him, an enjambed trio of tiny scenes:[20] first, Mark telling Marnie at dinner that she will raise the spectre of class at Wykwyn; then, on the deck, Marnie sarcastically reflecting on becoming 'a society hostess'; and finally, at dinner again, Mark regaling his bride about the fattid bugs. Quick dissolves link these moments, until we are brought to Mark reclining on the stateroom sofa in his amber silk pyjamas and robe,[21] reading *Animals of the Seashore* (1938) by Horace Gardiner Richards. He wants to find *some* subject that will appeal to her, says he theatrically (the distracted gentleman absorbed in his book, blithely unaware of the lateness and that he is shining a light). Marnie barks that she wants to go to bed and slams the door in his face. If, having withstood days of siege from this cavalier, she has lost her reserves, is weakened on every parapet, yet she treasures the fierce determination not to be victimised. Slamming that door is her penultimate gesture of defence.

But Mark's gun was cocked. An Arthurian gallant who has found his Damsel in distress, and agent, as he sees it, of her salvation, a man who knows in his heart that he loves her no matter what, he has worked to keep his hunger in check, to be – as he promised – 'kind'. What newly married man sits up and reads on his wedding nights? Slamming that door was more than an insult; it was a mocking shot across the bow. And Passion trumps Honour.

He leaps up, tosses Richards aside, runs to the bedroom door – to show the movement of Connery's legs, Hitchcock gives a full medium profile shot – opens, and enters. She is standing stock still in dim, oblique light, her hair brushed smooth (the way Bernice brushes Jessie Cotton's[22]), her hands at her sides, her eyes glazed and unwavering. 'If you don't want to go to bed, I wish you'd leave me alone,' says she, indignant. 'But I *do* wish to go to bed, Marnie.' The camera swings around to a three-quarter shot of Mark's glare, his curled lips, his martial reserve overcome by the force that vitiates the vow.

'No!'

Marnie in full-screen close shot: 'No!!!'

It is a broken scream full of bravery and fear,[23] at once the expression of a woman and the uncontrolled, unshaped bleat of a very little girl. His hands move up to tear off her nightdress, it drops around her feet.[24]

Rehearsing and shooting the nightgown shot: (top left) testing the tear-away garment designed by Edith Head, its shoulder straps cut and pre-taped; (top right) framing; (bottom) final shot

She is petrified. Seeing this, Mark snaps to, and with tender voice removes his robe to wrap her in it. He takes her face and kisses her ardently. We watch this Klimt[25] from above. We watch from below. Not a passionate and pleasurable but a protective kiss, to undo the past. Then her face over his shoulder, the eyes pulled all the way back to the furthest possible retreat, looking directly at the camera from their sepulchral chambers. His eyes again, dark, moving a little forward. We see her face as with perfectly guided fluidity she falls backwards. The camera pans to the porthole, moonlight on the 'phosphorescent sea' [Script, scene 333]. Fade.

Mastery

And is this, as some observers angrily claim, a rape? Does the honeymoon scene, with Mark's eager and uncontrolled passion, mar an otherwise polite and respectable psychological drama? Recognising that 'The desire to touch another human being who does not want to be touched animates the system of looking, desiring, and knowing, which always determined Hitchcock's cinema,' Joe McElhaney does not shirk from naming this 'rape sequence' a Hitchcockian set piece 'that joins ranks with the shower sequence from *Psycho*', even though Jay Presson Allen claimed 'that she never saw the sequence in those terms and that Hitchcock never used the word *rape* itself' during their script conferences (pp. 137, 133, 134).[26] William Rothman is convinced (as I am) that when we see the scene in its full context we have 'grounds for believing, as [Mark] does, that he is making love to her, not raping her. As Hitchcock films this moment, she even seems to move on her own accord to the bed, though backward, as if in a trance' (p. 415). In the view of Robin Wood, one of the few true champions of this film, who believed 'anyone who doesn't love *Marnie* doesn't really love Hitchcock' ('Looking': p. 84) and wrote, 'There is no more devastatingly beautiful scene in the whole of Hitchcock' (*Films*: p. 188), Mark is raping his wife but doesn't know it (Allen, 'Interview': p. 20). Evan Hunter, who shrank from writing this scene, recollects, 'When I told Jay Presson Allen how much his description of that scene had bothered me, she said, "You just got bothered by the scene that was his reason for making the movie. You just wrote your ticket back to New York"' (p. 76). He claims further that in a taped working session, after noting that 'you follow her head as he forces her down onto the bed, and you know—', Hitchcock turned off the machine and 'described the rape scene' (in Spoto: p. 497). While in paperwork filed with the Production Code Administration, Hitchcock specified the film included no rape, the censor insisted on carping: 'Mark's actions could almost be described as an action of rape ... His stripping Marnie nude could not be approved' (Shurlock to Robertson).

Let us imagine – or believe, for in the end it comes to the same thing – that a person's sole and simple law at each moment is to fully *be*, to feel and interpret without obstruction, to sense natural rhythm expressed through the movement and utterance of others; then to respond with unfettered honesty and directness upon a breath, as though censorship, politics, expediency, and deceit did not exist. Interrelationship is play, and the individual requires the freedom and space to act without inhibition and with full reassurance of support. This is the portion of our social landscape devoted to our aboriginal nature. Language is dissociated from this real state of human feeling and instantaneous need. Words are all insufficient, all circumlocutions. No tongue seems truly our own, and every usage is in some way forced. The best one can do is poetry, and the best of poetry is silence. Now see Mark and Marnie's challenge as they work through their moment. They have achieved what amounts to a lot of navigation, yet have skirted the actual position, the trap, in which their marriage has placed them.

What precisely can Mark take her to mean when Marnie bellows, 'No!'? 'I don't want to have sex with you'? – this she has said before, proclaims as a motto, notwithstanding the current of experience. This woman in extremis, whose every statement has been a lie, who has lived a life of masquerade: is she suddenly to be taken at face value because she has negated, of all things, sex? Note the four sharp ripostes arranged in alternation by Hitchcock: (a) Marnie slamming the door in Mark's face; (b) Mark throwing open the door and walking in; (c) Marnie shrieking, 'No!'; (d) Mark dragging her nightgown down. Convention places (b) as a response to (a) and (d) as a response to (c), but could (d) not rebound (a), and (c) not reflect (b)? She humiliates him with the door so he humiliates her with the gown (then instantly regrets his barbaric impulse). He barges in when she wants solitude and she forces him back with her trumpet cry. The voice of that 'No!' is both adult and childish, the self of the film's present and the self of the hidden time that we have not yet discovered in the closet of Marnie's obscure childhood. When Mark kissed her in his office during the thunderstorm, and again in the stables at Wykwyn, we saw her fondness for sex, at least with him. Is it possible that Mark's bursting into the ship's bedroom invokes *another* intrusive male? Could the 'No!' be for someone else? Could the 'No!' be emanating, totally acousmatic,[27] from another Marnie?

Powerless

No film is only what we see on the screen. Consider cuts and elisions. In *Marnie* – as in his other work, especially when he was benefiting from big-studio production in the United States – Hitchcock might elaborate scenes in a script, cast them carefully, rehearse and shoot them, but omit them from the final cut. There were numerous such deletions from this film, but a telling example involved the *droit du seigneur*, an ancient ritualised arrangement – acknowledged in the *Epic of Gilgamesh* – whereby the king or most elevated local patriarch takes unto himself every local virgin on her wedding night. In scene [122], set outside Ward's office just after 'Mary Taylor' has been hired (and shot by Hitchcock on 27 and 29 October 1963 at Universal Stage 21), Artie Nelson comments archly about Mark:

ARTIE: You mean I'm up against whatdy-call-it? [an approximate
         pronunciation] ... *Droit de seigneur?* (leans on MARNIE'S desk) Know
         what I mean? Like has Rutland got you all staked out, honey, or is
         there any chance for us rabble?

Gone is the speech but not the theme, which is the power of men.
In patriarchal capitalism, is not every man a Gilgamesh unto himself?
Artie is signalling what the film shows anyway, Mark's high status (as
inheritor of Rutland's) relative to his own (as a mere office boy) and
that any male might fancy Mary Taylor on first sight. To make a
flirtatious moment here is to invoke fun and fulfilment. But to couch
the invocation in the *droit du seigneur* is to render Artie, beyond a
well-educated quipper, a harbinger of class difference, the absolute
grounding of all the action in this film. Artie will appear again, with a
self-conscious meekness that keeps the resonances of the *droit du
seigneur* fully in place.

Artie (Linden Chiles) spieling Marnie

Consider *Marnie* as an essay on verticality: Marnie's powerlessness in relation to the Rutlands' high puissance, Bernice's *lumpen* brittleness and unfulfilled yearning, her continual search for *decency* in an attempt to raise herself above the disapprovably low while being trapped in passivity (emphasised by her limp). We see Bernice's repressed but craven want when Marnie gifts her the fur stole, then hear her sanctimonious sermon about corrupt money and male pollution, a pious struggle for high ground in the invisible territory of correctness and propriety (vitally guarded values for which the very rich need spare no time). For this 'decent' audience, Marnie has fostered a chain of illusions concerning another *seigneur*, 'Mr Pemberton', from whom she ostensibly receives bonuses and special rewards: this system of accounting for her deviant behaviour (see Scott and Lyman) normalises her status when in truth she is a rank thief.[28] What is interesting about 'Mr Pemberton' is the sexual self-allusion that resides beneath Marnie's characterisation of him – what Bill Krohn refers to much more broadly as Hitchcock's underlying 'cartoon'[29]: Marnie has a fictional, second self, a working girl so sexually alluring that her employer is lavish with his attentions. Of course, in the honeymoon sequence, this fictional second self becomes startlingly real to her. The stunned expression on her face as Mark lowers her to the bed is partly her realisation that she has invented her own fate.

But even another layer of 'underpainting' lingers below Marnie's reactions with Mark. That broken squeal, 'No!', echoes a child beneath the adult Marnie, one more 'cartoon'. She, not the grown woman, is the frozen, almost catatonic, presence in his arms. It is no simple matter to read and digest this scene, and considerably more than Mark's domination is in process here. There is no escape from the fact that he is become the camera, the viewer's stand-in. Indeed, as Raymond Bellour observes, 'Hitchcock becomes a sort of double of Mark', and he means Hitchcock, that 'man with the movie camera, the kino-eye: the author-enunciator' (pp. 73, 68). We are all now 'very much wanting to go to bed' with Marnie and being held back.

Shooting Marnie falling back
to the bed

Mark is become the camera.
Connery resting during the
production of the honeymoon scene

At dawn, she will escape the *seigneur* and attempt suicide in the ship's pool, but he will save her. Hitchcock fades from the porthole at night to a shot of the same porthole the next morning,[30] then pans to the bed where Mark, awakening, sees she's gone. How simple, one might think, to match one porthole shot with another, with rear-projection plates of the sea outside, one for moonlight and another for the overcast morning. But Hitchcock always has a surprise: At night the ripples of the water are travelling rightward onscreen; by morning they have reversed direction. Has the ship turned? Or have we?

Connery and the second unit shooting the shipboard pool rescue in San Francisco, 14 March 1964. Alma Reville is at extreme right. Immediately after the session, the ship was scuttled

3 Confederacy

Culturally and mythically, *Marnie* presents a tableau darker and
more historically fraught than its surface story suggests.

Begin with Mark Rutland and his father, established heralds of
an entrenched and unrelenting capitalism. Bored with business, the
old man let the company slide. On taking over, his hard-nosed son
'*retired* ... three board members, the acting president, the president's
secretary, and the secretary's secretary'. But Mark is also a reservoir
of principles: learning of Marnie's previous thefts, and 'fighting a
powerful impulse to beat the hell out of' her, he recognises that he'd
be 'criminally and morally responsible' if he let her go. 'Sooner or
later you'd have gone to jail or have been cornered in an office by

Who needs a wig? Connery's hairpieces for the film, made on Baker Street, London,
cost a little over £75 (Robertson to Donnelly, 29 November 1963) and were returned
to him as a gift from Hitchcock when shooting was done (Robertson to Connery)

some angry old bull of a businessman out to take what he figured was coming to him,' he pontificates on the honeymoon. 'I'd say you needed all the help you could get.' The Rutland sanctuary reflecting money but lacking opulence, one can perhaps fathom Marnie's eagerness to be away from it. When the sanctimonious Strutt recognises her at a soirée there, her default reaction is to pack her bags, but savvy Mark has no qualms about buying him off – Robin Wood sees Mark 'acting for life, against the deadening self-righteousness of conventional morality' (*Films*: p. 189) – buying off all her victims, indeed: this is the vital umbrella of his protection.

By contrast, Bernice Edgar's house seems all incipient decay. Her dress is clean but cheap, Edwin Landseer's dog portrait 'Dignity and Impudence' reproduced on the wall suggests art at a distance (and a lost age of decadence[31]), and assembled bric-a-brac betoken not so much spending ability as the valuation of preciosity. Bernice 'is always in danger of expulsion from the temple' (Allen, Script). The past is infused into every object and moment through a potently seductive, ghostly presence. Bernice has always been poor – '*Grindingly* poor', Marnie tells Mark – yet her house means to radiate a warm and welcoming spirit even if in truth it is a *terrain vague*, *heimlich* and haunted, an 'interior emptied of [its] occupants' (Deleuze: p. 16). Bernice's home and Wykwyn occupy different geographies.

These two production photographs, taken moments apart, illustrate how Hitchcock and his cinematographer Robert Burks worked at lighting nuances to achieve the 'ghostly' effect with Bernice

North/South

In his discussion of the post-bellum American South, Wolfgang
Schivelbusch differentiates between a North imaged as wilderness,
where hard work was valorised 'as the key to salvation', and the
'non-Puritan South with its friendlier climate' as 'heir to the
Elizabethan conception of the New World as a garden, an earthly
paradise'; here was devotion to the 'epicurean enjoyment of the
garden that Providence had bestowed' (*Culture of Defeat*: p. 40).
He quotes William Hepworth Dixon's observation that Southerners
felt 'the English were of nearer kin to them than their Yankee
brethren', while in the North,

The valuation of preciosity

the men being all intent on their affairs, they neither hunted, fished, nor danced; they talked of scarcely anything but their mills, their mines, their roads, their fisheries; they were always eager, hurried, and absorbed, as though the universe hung upon their arms, and they feared to let it fall (p. 41).

Strutt is one of these anxious Northerners and Mark, who traps and tames Southern beasts and writes casually about them, might have been his brother-in-arms. As he must confess to Marnie, 'I've caught something *really* wild this time … I've tracked you and caught you, and by God, I'm going to keep you.'

Yet it was Scotland, not England, tightly bonded to the ante-bellum South, Scotland the 'model of an anti-England that young America could emulate' (Schivelbusch: p. 48), Scotland as evidenced in the gracious brogue that Connery brings to his performance.[32] If in Wykwyn the Rutlands are in something of a rut, this may be because the family, originally Scottish and friendly to the American South, has over-accommodated to the business demands of the victorious North, has been trading with the same people Marnie has had to rob, her bona fides not standing up as the Rutland credentials do.

As an inheritor of Southern losses, Bernice has picked up Northern Puritan sternness: nervousness about God and his constant observation, refusal to '[prize] the classics of antiquity above the King James Bible' (Schivelbusch: p. 41). Yet at the same time she possesses poise and staunch dignity (thus 'Dignity and Impudence' on her wall), placing self-respect and 'a good name' above all things. Bernice is a prisoner of war, a Southerner in captivity to her own defeat, holding herself responsible for the 'dead-end path' on which she is trapped (p. 57). Past battle now, past action, Bernice has dropped onto the plain of pure reflection: as the historian Edward A. Pollard noted, 'All that is left the South is "the war of ideas"' (quoted in Schivelbusch: p. 59).

Marnie has escaped the confines of the maternal 'prison' and 'path'. Mark, for all his shrewdness and make-do, has inherited – perhaps from the aristocracy of his forebears – a sense of ease.

Never busy, he always has 'time for wit, for compliment, for small talk' (Dixon quoted in Schivelbusch: p. 41). His gracefulness is at war with his no-nonsense practicality. He is a Northerner gone south; just as Bernice and Marnie, Southerners gone north, are epitomes of an idle life turned perforce to stressful labour, self-consciousness, piety, and deceit.

Subtexts

If, as Marnie's thieving comes to Mark's attention and he must figure out what to do, we concentrate on her story with its twists and suspensions, thrills and provocations, we gain only a kleptomaniac and a man in love, a self-proclaimed 'liar and thief' and a lover of lies and theft. How might Mark save Marnie from herself? What will happen – to their love, to Marnie's future, to Mark's goodwill – when he uncovers the sombre secret of her past, the reason for her constant flights from the police, moral goodness, honest relations, and the male touch? These challenges can indeed be found in the film. But in writing and thinking about Hitchcock, it is too misleading to revel in so-called 'Hitchcockian' themes – his obsessions with blondes, mistaken guilt, and the macabre – and too easy to acknowledge only events and expressions. What if we view *Marnie* without being constrained by the official 'thievery' story? Suddenly we note all of this:

That the handbag floating away from the camera in the first two shots of the film is coloured vibrant gold. Any handbag would have had 'handbagness', but this one, while also signing feminine lucre in motion, has a signal paradisical tropicality.

That Marnie has stabled Forio in the Virginia countryside,[33] with its rolling fields and time-gone-by beauty.

That whistling is a latent theme. In his private reflections, the cupidinous Strutt, describing her to detectives, is still (wolf-)whistling about good-looking 'Marion Holland', who robbed him. The unheard whistle returns with Artie at Rutland's, similarly besmitten on first glance; and indirectly through Lil, whose jealous possessiveness is

reflecting 'Mrs Taylor's' whistlable allure when she asks Mark pointedly, 'Who's the dish?' Imperious and demanding even at her young age, Jessie 'whistles for' Bernice as though to a servant.

That Jessie Cotton speaks with a drawl.

That Bernice drawls, too.[34] 'She is common in an essentially Southern way,' wrote Allen, 'a way which implies ignorance and material deprivation rather than a purely physical, generic vulgarity' (Script). As the film moves toward its conclusion, this drawl will be intensively pronounced. Remarkable in their early encounter is that Marnie does *not* drawl but uses a crisp, Northern elocution – too crisp, perhaps, as though learned by rote. Mark notices her 'careful grammar … quiet good manners … where did you learn them?' And she answers ambiguously, 'From my betters' (those who are better than I am; those who have been betting on me: later, on the phone to her mother, we hear her say, 'I *am* still a little hoarse' but it sounds like 'a little horse').

Martin Gabel as Strutt

That of all treats Bernice could be preparing for Jessie, she is baking a pecan pie. 'Pecans are, to my mind, the most Southern of nuts,' writes a supreme authority on American cooking and the South (Claiborne, *Cooking*: p. 317); 'they are probably more American than apple pie' (Claiborne, *Encyclopedia*: p. 328). Emphasis is given to this prize when Marnie, provoking a small argument about money, gets slapped by her mother in the kitchen, knocking the dish of unshelled pecans all over the floor. More emphatically still, after offering to gather the nuts, Marnie is sent for a nap upstairs and Bernice says she'll get Jessie to do the work: 'After all,' snips Marnie in the doorway (in a line added to the script), 'it *is* Jessie's pecan pie, isn't it.' We never see the confection itself: it is what pecan pie symbolises, not pecan pie, Hitchcock is invoking.

That, caught by Mark after robbing his safe, Marnie makes a slip of the tongue as she fabricates her Californian biography, pronouncing the word 'insurance' with a stress on the first syllable, as people do (Mark points out) only in the South.

Pecan spill

That in Mark's office, before sitting to type his manuscript on *Arboreal Predators of the Brazilian Rain Forest* (of all subjects), Marnie notices that stunning photograph of Sophie. She and the cat share ferociously intelligent eyes, and a certain pungent beauty. The picture thus identifies Marnie as much as the cat, and the jaguarundi is a creature of the southern hemisphere. (Animal bonding continues through the film, as Marnie connects with Forio and the pathetic fox hunted to its death; and is reflected by the brazen little terrier in the Landseer picture.)

That Marnie's illegal adventures took place in Boston, Detroit, Elizabeth, New Jersey, and New York, all bastions of Northern enterprise.

That Marnie's deep history, as symbolised through her memory, seems cloistered in Southern tones, with young Bernice garbed to suggest the New Orleans prostitutes photographed by E. J. Bellocq.

That until her culminating fall into Mark's shepherding care after her reborn memory, Marnie glitters and shines by bravely lying. What her lies cover: the past (as far as she can know it), her desire, her intentions, her awareness, her real feelings for people, her mother's very existence. Not Marnie's thieving but her deceit seems the centre of this tale. I point out in *An Eye for Hitchcock* that Marnie is 'whistling Dixie' – betraying, falsifying, misleading, avoiding the truth. This 'whistling' (silently implied by the undertone whistlings I mention above) betokens her falseness, since in American popular culture, as Hitchcock and his screenwriter knew, those who speak the truth 'ain't just whistlin' Dixie'. *Whistling* 'Dixie' is for those who don't know the words, don't recognise an anthem to the defeated South. 'Wish I was in the land of cotton/Old times there are not forgotten.' But if superficially Marnie is 'whistling Dixie' – telling lies – in her depths she is singing it, since her actions avenge against the economic centres of the North. And Bernice's house – the land of Cotton: Marnie does wish she could be there with old times not forgotten. But loyal as she is, she is banished and without a past.

Mark's sole project in *Marnie* is to rescue this girl from her amnesia, help her locate the memories of 'old times' so she can live in the present. He must time-travel with no map. Clues not placed in the narrative so Mark can cut a path to Marnie's rescue are there so that viewers can share willingly in his concern. We must come to love Marnie because of her blazing pride, her animality, the elemental warmth buried within the frozen sheath of her fear.

Fox

The fox hunt is an invention of the sixteenth century that blossomed among the English aristocracy in the Victorian and Edwardian ages. Because the aristocracy behind them is not English, the Rutland

Louise Latham as the young Bernice, off camera

hunt[35] is a show of propriety, but the old man does fancy horses and Marnie does, too. (Is it a test or a revelation that Mark's first dedicated necking session with her is in the Wykwyn stables?) When she is given to ride with the hunt,[36] the physical challenges are no obstruction to her. There are marvellous shots of her galloping across the fields and taking the jumps, including some masterfully executed effects shots of Marnie, Lil, and other riders against the field of the hunting group.[37]

Marnie's crisis is produced on the turn of an eye. Coming upon the prey with the other riders and watching their too obvious blood lust, she realises how savage will be the killing and how hopeless the poor creature's fate.[38] We do not see the dogs lunge, but we hear them. A rider's pinks shock Marnie into one of her fits, with the screen again soaked in pulsating red. But it is a double shock that has beset her. First, the blood. Secondly, her profound identification with the victimised animal. All too plainly, Marnie can see how society is

A real Pennsylvania hunt staged as background for Marnie's flight

little more than a fox hunt, with the callous, brave, unforgiving, and desperate (Strutt and Co.) ganging up on the weak, vulnerable, feelingful, and innocent. In this way, Schivelbusch recounts, the North 'ganged up' on the South. 'Shermanising'[39] helped create a state of affairs in which 'a fifth of Mississippi's first postwar state budget was devoted to the production of prosthetic limbs for those maimed in the fighting' (*Culture of Defeat*: p. 38). No prostheses for Marnie, however. She is the fox, her life a race with the hounds behind. (Her vulnerability at the challenging, pursuing gaze of others finds a stunning example in a sequence I address in the next chapter.)

Production notes

One reviewer drew attention to Hitchcock's 'loving care' in having the hunt photographed 'in country which actually *looks* like Pennsylvania' (Wharton: p. 437). Essentially, two kinds of images are intermingled in the editing for the hunt. Long shots of an actual

Eyeing the fox

event, made, indeed, in Pennsylvania, show the melange of actions and personnel, the organic connection between the dogs, horses, humans, and fleeing fox. Process shots give point of view or close detail, and these are typically executed with the horse and rider on a large treadmill, the animal held in position by guide cords attached to its bridle and held by wranglers on the right and left sides. Behind the horse/rider combination there is a screen, usually about five-by-seven feet, on which footage of the passing countryside, shot in advance by a second-unit team, is rear-projected in sync with the foreground action. If the cinematographer takes care lighting the set-up, the melding of foreground and background 'realities' appears seamless and whole. The rear projection needs to be lined up so that there is perfectly clear focus and no untoward hot spot in the centre. The aperture mechanism of the projector and that of the camera

This production photograph from the process stage shows Diane Baker mounted, her horse on a treadmill and guided at the mouth. Behind, on the rear-projection screen, is an exceptionally crisp plate showing other riders (from a real hunt)

must be in absolute match. Further, the performers' gestures must relate in a believable way to what is going on behind them in the shot, while in practice they are unable to see it. If an elaborate treadmill shot is required, involving multiple devices or numerous riders, or if for other reasons the background image must be larger, the triple-head projector[40] can overlap three identical copies of the image simultaneously, thereby gaining contrast and brilliance.

Marnie turns Forio and flees from the imperilled fox, but she is finally unable to negotiate a stone wall and the horse takes a bad fall, breaking a leg. Extricating herself, Marnie runs up to the nearby farmhouse and begs for a gun. The farmer's wife (Meg Wyllie) is reticent until Lil comes up to give the Rutland nod. Marnie points the gun stolidly in macro-close-up (away from the audience), firing one ringing shot. 'There,' as though soothing a child, 'There now.'[41] Something in Hedren's posture stiffens on the fade. She is on autopilot now, her face mortified and cold, inert. Through some inconceivable magic her spirit has evaporated. This is a triumph of film-making craft, with the long slightly dishevelled hair by Virginia Darcy, the tautly fitting riding garb by Edith Head that emphasises the frame of Hedren's body, the pallid make-up by Jack Barron,[42] and the extremely restrained, 'technical' Hedren performance.[43]

(left) Hedren is on Forio on the process stage; (right) from the same stage, without the rear projection

The last shots of the sequence [457]–[469] – involving Marnie and that fateful wall; Marnie fallen; and Marnie at the farmhouse – were started at Disney's Golden Oak Ranch[44] on 3 February 1964 and finished over the next two days. Transparency plates for Marnie's perspective as Forio approaches the stone wall were made in the same location on 24 February, utilising Forio and his equine double. Further process shots, including the foxhole itself, were made on Stage 32 at Universal on 27 February. The same stage was used on 9, 10, 11 and 13 March for open-field process shots, countryside process shots, shots of Marnie leaving the hunt, shots of her leaping a brook and a wall, and a point-of-view jump shot (with May Boss as riding double, and for which Robert Burks borrowed Paramount's diminishing lens [Burks to Bishop]).

Marnie heads for Ward's office, opens his safe, stands frozen and transfixed, paralysed and vacant. She tries to reach in but cannot. Mark is suddenly behind her, urging her to continue.

Forio is in rear projection

'You're not stealing ... if you want the money, take it.' Then the bomb: 'We're going to Baltimore to see your mother.' She screams 'No' again, almost exactly as before, but we do not want her to have her way any more than Mark does when he says 'Yes'.

Tea

Earlier, however, after the typing session and their visit to the Atlantic City track (about which more anon), Mark and Marnie step into a mad little tea party. He has brought her to Wykwyn (where, Deborah Thomas suggests, he is 'unhappy' [p. 118]). The old man is in pontifical mode, boldly announcing that his son brought 'Mrs Taylor' out not to see the house but to meet him. As for riding, he is bluntly philosophical, if riddling: 'The best thing in the world for the inside of a man or woman is the outside of a horse.'

Frustrated Lil is set to challenge 'Mrs Taylor' for Mark's attentions, feigning a sprained wrist and asking the visitor to please pour – a condescending test of breeding and style (which Marnie does not fail).[45] Lil's clear expectation is that by committing a faux pas[46] Marnie will degrade herself and openly demonstrate her unfitness to couple with the family scion. If Marnie misses Lil's move, Mark doesn't. Taking 'Mrs Taylor' to the stables, he blocks Lil from joining them, ordering her to stay and pour his dad some more tea. 'I *can't*!' protests Lil, holding up the wrist. But, one up on her, Mark mocks:

> When duty whispers low,
> Thou must,
> Then youth replies,
> I can!

He and Marnie have vanished by the time Lil, her eyes on fire, calls out, 'Rat-fink! And you misquoted!'[47]

The quotation/misquotation is another apparently decorative, but structurally vital, fillip. Mark's lines, from Ralph Waldo Emerson's 'Voluntaries', were written during and about the Civil War

and originally published in 1863 in *The Atlantic*. Addressing the widespread disaffection of youth living in a culture without essential values, this work asks what charge could possibly make them willing to 'break sharply off their jolly games … forsake their comrades … quit proud homes' in order 'to hazard all in Freedom's fight'.

The words of a Northern poet, a man who believes in the redeeming infinitude of the individual, yet who here supports the call to arms of an army that was waging against the South a *total* campaign, one in which General Philip Henry Sheridan recommended, 'The people must be left nothing but their eyes to weep with over the war' (Schivelbusch, *Culture of Defeat*: p. 39). This, Mark knows too well, is Lil's attitude toward Marnie. At this tea party, under the pretext of sociability and cake, we find a Mason–Dixon line. Mark is ultimately on Marnie's side, devoted to helping her, and loyal (thus, a traitor). As for Marnie, the move to Rutland's was more perilous than it seemed. She has fallen among the enemy.

'Rat-fink!'

4 Face-off

Marnie's realisation of her own identity as victim, central to this film, her wounded sense that she is a fox set upon by hungry hounds, is beautifully prepared in an early elaboration when, having learned that she is fond of horses, Mark escorts her to the Atlantic City racecourse. A devotedly classical composer, Hitchcock always prepares his harmonic resolutions and cadences in advance: every significance has its anticipation, every shot its economy and informative value. To examine the racetrack sequence closely is to see into Hitchcock's vibrant, self-critical method, to be shown how he puts on show Marnie's being on show. Set out in Allen's final shooting script (29 October 1963), the filmic grammar is typically crisp and unambiguous, but Hitchcock felt entirely free to add or delete while he worked. Moreover, material was tightened, shaped, disambiguated, and clarified in post-production. This examination can show the depth of Hitchcock's interest in Marnie as the object of a generally aggressive critical gaze. But we can see, too, the meticulous grammar of his shot scripting and his fluid, incisive, practical editorial process as he works during shooting to condense, elide, smooth, and tighten the work even further.

The looking to which I refer in this sequence, as emblematic of the central looking which has traumatised Marnie, perhaps transcends the form that Laura Mulvey writes about when she discusses Freud's scopophilia. Neither 'taking other people as objects, subjecting them to a controlling and curious gaze' for pleasure, nor revelling narcissistically in one's own gazing power (see Mulvey: pp. 16–19) quite approach the alienating, systematising, reducing, and socially organised gaze that has put Marnie in flight and brought on her continuing fearful sense of being discovered in masquerade.

For introduction, the script has a long 'comprehensive' shot of the filled grandstand [192].[48] Then, past some standing patrons, a forward zoom into [193] a close shot of a man (Milton Selzer) watching something undisclosed. George Tomasini's final edit adds an unscripted insert [192-0], showing the track's floral centrepiece: 'ATLANTIC CITY RACE COURSE'. Further, the Second Unit made [192] during a real race, the horses pummelling past the camera at trackside – a good action break yet also swift and direct indication of Marnie's passion and viewers' position. In practice [193] was a little different: the man is in medium shot, with a woman behind him[49] staring through binoculars in the same direction as his gaze – a Hitchcockian tickle, to position our awareness through visual alliteration: this scene is only overtly about horses and racing; more deeply it is about using the eyes.

From the man's point of view comes [194], a (Second Unit) medium shot of the turf club area. In close-up [Script 195], he telescopes his newspaper and brings it up to his eye (but the film

Mark and Marnie through the newspaper roll

shows the rolled-up paper ready in his hand as he raises it[50]).
[196]: Through the 'aperture' of the newspaper we discover the
object of his attention, Mark and Marnie at a table (with Mark, in
another of Hitchcock's visual rhymes, staring off at the track through
his own binoculars and Marnie looking back into the stands).
Gazer and target. To seal the Kuleshovian gazer–object–gazer
construction (see Truffaut: pp. 214–15), another close-up of the man
[197] lowering the newspaper roll and starting to walk off,
presumably in their direction. Note how Hitchcock tells his viewer
what it is necessary to know at each developing instant in the story:
this man, whoever he is, has seen something and is on the prowl, thus
Mark and Marnie are vulnerable to oversight.

A close-profile two-shot [198] gives opportunity for their banter
about betting on a horse named Lemon Pudding, and Mark exits to
'get on him' (preparation for a linguistic joke, because in the following
scenes at Wykwyn his charming father will chide Mark for not riding;
'get on him' is a purely economic gesture for Mark, not just at the
track, where he may not ride, but even when he *does* mount a horse
after nabbing Marnie later on [see image on p. 24]). With Mark gone,
the man enters the frame and purrs to Marnie, 'You're Peggy
Nicholson, aren't you? Remember me?' She looks up. Hitchcock needs
more intrusion, more information, more angle than this coherent script
offers: he splits [198] into a second shot [198-1], unscripted, giving a
face-on view of Marnie so that the man now enters from screen left, his
rolled-up newspaper visible at her shoulder height as stand-in for its
user. Making this addition opens up the interaction, allows for a full
view of Marnie's surprised face when she hears his unknown voice.
Hitchcock also transposes the man's last line, 'Remember me?', into
the upcoming [199], where we see his face directly as he utters it.
Again, a joke: Marnie as 'Mrs Taylor' remembers nothing, while
'backstage' she *does* remember him and can't have him know.
The viewer remembers him, too, having just watched a number of
shots Marnie didn't see. Through this little manoeuvre, viewer
consciousness is aligned with the 'backstage' Marnie, forced now to

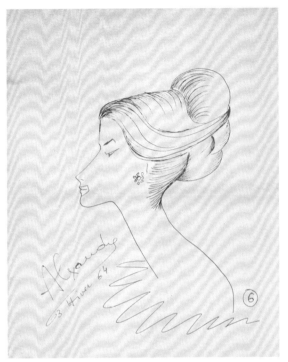

Hairstyling and star construction: one of more than twenty designs commissioned by Hitchcock from Alexandre of Paris for Hedren

Alexandre's assistant, Gwendolyn (Annie Le Couteux), testing a hairstyle on Hedren

strategise a way out of this situation. She is on constant show, unavoidably disporting past identities on that pretty face.

On recognising women by their faces: this is crucial not only for *Marnie* but for the business of cinema generally. What are stars, after all, but people who have become bankable on the basis of their familiarity? In this interchange Hedren, whose star image was thoroughly groomed by Hitchcock,[51] is playing none other than a star, Marnie, who cannot lose her image. Marnie's attempts at camouflage always involve hairdos and hair re-colourings, but this relentless man, who will not take the fedora from his head, cares about facial features, not hair. With stars it is the same: no matter their make-up and styling they must, like Marnie, read immediately as being always and perdurably themselves.

Shot [199] is a head-and-shoulders Dutch-angle close-up of the man looming over Marnie, the camera taking her position at table height and shooting upward into his neutral face. A 'Dutch-angle' shot is one taken with the camera looking upward or downward at its subject.[52] [200] is a long medium shot, reprising the angle of [198-1]: the man affirms and Marnie denies the label he wishes to affix. Hitchcock inserts an unscripted Dutch angle [200-1] looking down at Marnie from the man's point of view; daylight streams onto her auburn hair and into her clear eyes as she rebuffs him. Another unscripted insert of a reciprocal Dutch angle upwards toward him [200-2], as he says he was 'pretty sure' she was Peggy Nicholson. Another unscripted insert of Marnie, the same Dutch angle looking down [200-3]: 'I'm sorry, you've made a mistake, I am not Miss Nichols.' 'Nicholson', he says, both to correct and to persist. Nor will this hound be put off the scent. In another inserted upward Dutch angle [200-4], he presses that Frank Abernathy introduced them in Detroit. An unscripted pause as, in a downward Dutch angle [200-5], she stares up at him; then back to him from her point of view [200-6]: 'Frank Abernathy,' says he. 'You remember Frank!' (A wicked smile.) Back to a high Dutch angle of Marnie [200-7], turning her eyes up 'to think': 'No, I do not remember

Matching Dutch angles [199] and [200-1]. Note how Hitchcock cheats the camera placement; in his gaze (bottom) Marnie is drawn forward, while in hers (top) he is pushed away

anyone named Frank Abernathy. I have *never* known anyone named Frank Abernathy. Now will you please go?' The reverse Dutch angle again [200-8], with his eyes narrowing a little in suspicion: 'Come on now, honey, you're trying to pull my leg, aren't you?' All these Dutch angles in a vertical tennis game, why? To indicate reality, because we see the man standing and Marnie sitting? Or, does Hitchcock have the man standing and Marnie sitting so that he can effect all these Dutch angles? They produce a delicious vertiginousness, make us 'look up' and 'look down', as Scottie Ferguson does in *Vertigo* (1958). They produce tension, pressing Marnie with the weight of the man's figure and supposition. And given her relative powerlessness they demonstrate her indomitable spirit for unflinching performance. She is always bravely – but perforcedly – on show.

Mark has entered off camera left (in the same shot). His deep, resonant voice: 'Why should any young lady want to pull *your* leg?' A medium three-shot [200-9], with Marnie seated right and the two males standing left. The man is easing off, claiming he thought he recognised her:

MARK: Did he recognise you?

MARNIE: No.

MARK (to man, with a directive voice):   You did not recognise her.

The man still won't budge. 'I said I *thought* I recognised her ... I *said* I'm sorry.' Mark's voice razor sharp: 'Good for you. You've apologised nicely. You may go' – the full patrician treatment of the hoi polloi, forcing an end to the encounter.

Through this balance-destroying game of intercalated upward and downward gazes, and the vertical structure of class relations invoked as Mark dismisses the stranger from a social height, Marnie is silent and lost, since she is and is not Peggy Nicholson at once, in the same way that she is and is not the Marnie we and so many other people see. Her sense of self rides on what others think – a well-received concept[53] here narratively tailored in a demonstration that is completely visual.

Creative removals

A scripted medium shot of Mark sitting down again [201] was to follow. 'Who's your fan?,' he asks Marnie, and she muses in close-up [202], 'I just seem to have one of *those* faces.' In practice, Hitchcock conflated the above two shots and had Hedren delivering her response to Mark with her back to camera. He then cuts to a reverse shot showing her donning her coat [new 202]. In a medium two-shot [202-1], as at the start of the sequence, she asks if they can visit the paddock to see her favourite, Telepathy.

From here on, a considerable portion of the shooting script is entirely voided, with new set-ups and transitions more or less improvised. To plumb the director's intent, it helps to see what is lost:

- Scripted [203], a close-up of Mark watching Marnie as she notes that the horses are at the gate. (*Nice, but irrelevant; it isn't the race we care about, it's Marnie.*)
- Marnie, close up [204], touting Lemon Pudding – 'He'll win' – with the camera dollying in as she looks at the track. (*Lemon Pudding, for all his worth to her, is meaningless to Hitchcock's story.*)
- A big head shot of Marnie [205] looking out to the track, then turning and looking past the camera (*That she's interested in something else right now we already know.*)

Retained is a medium shot of the man looking offscreen right [202-2], from which direction Mark and Marnie enter, breeze past him, then exit as he turns to look after them. (*This allows us to see their dignity and his uncertainty.*) Hitchcock cuts now to the scripted [215, below], entirely eliding a visually very dramatic, but also overstated, arrangement involving all of the following:

- [206] a close-up of the man looking downward, *dissolving* to:
- [207] a profile close-up of Marnie, looking past the camera; then
- [208] a close-up again of the man looking down, *dissolving* to:

- [209] another (emphatic) close-up of Marnie turning and looking past the camera; then
- [210] yet another close-up of the man, still looking at her, *dissolving* to:
- [211] yet another close-up of Marnie, who turns and looks past the camera; then
- [212] one more close-up of the man staring at her, again *dissolving*.

Seven shots of staring and four *dissolves*: more than a direct reciprocity between her gazes off and his gazes at her, this cut dispenses with a temporal and spatial extenuation of the man's gaze, as though he sees the past and present – Peggy Nicholson and Marnie – in one melting cliché. The arrangement permitted a double vision, the lingering of one shot into the opening of a second, and in this way produced *and also invoked* doubleness (Marnie's numerous doublings in the film), the dissolve working to confuse the gaze, melt character, and above all, enrich our focus upon Marnie. Hitchcock eliminated the dissolves in a memo to his editor on 24 March 1964. We are already attached to Marnie; and the doubling did not need this excessive emphasis.

Also elided:

- [213], a medium shot of Mark raving about Marnie's talent for picking horses; brief talk about one named Telepathy (*her talent is irrelevant; and she mentions Telepathy elsewhere*); then:
- [214] another (blatantly emphatic) close-up of the man aggressively watching Mark and Marnie, as her consciousness develops that she is the object of his gaze (*we know this already*).

The shot Hitchcock picks up, [215], is a high establishing view of the paddock ring, reprising Marnie's yearning to see Telepathy and generally refracting the desire to see – in this case, to see Marnie. Strutt and the other Northern entrepreneurs want to see Marnie, and now, *Marnie* itself is Hitchcock's paddock, and our heroine is the telepathic wonder at its centre.

[216], a close shot of Mark and Marnie as they watch the equine parade, has been cut. Instead [new 216] Hitchcock shot a medium view of Mark and Marnie (with rear projection) walking toward the camera, then [216-1] a reverse medium shot of a horse parading by. [217] becomes explicit, with Mark suggesting the horse is Marnie's 'old friend, Telepathy'. Back to the horse [217-1]. MARK (off camera): 'Yes, Number 8.' Marnie stares in an extreme close-up [218]; and in a medium shot from her point of view [219] we look upon the flanks of the horse and rider, his silks white with red polka dots. A blaring musical cue.

[220], a tight close-up reverse of Marnie seeing, then quickly turning: 'Again the SCREEN IS SUFFUSED WITH A RED GLOW which quickly FADES subliminally.'[54] Marnie is immobilised. An inserted two-shot [220-1], Mark looking down at his racing form, Marnie looking off-left, past his shoulder – MARK (offscreen): 'What is it? What's the matter?' She curtly says, 'Don't bet him. …

Offensive silks in [219]

He's wall-eyed. Can we go now?' Mark and Marnie depart from the paddock but not before we see [220-2] an inserted unscripted close-up of the jockey in his red polka dots jostling in the saddle, and return to [220-3] Mark taking 'one last inquisitive look over his shoulder. What was wrong? ... What did she see?'

Hitchcock has brought us to the paddock to see Telepathy's rider's silks, a surprise for the viewer and for Marnie. The effect is to link us with her, and momentarily to keep us separate from Mark, who does not fathom what is going on.

The staring man is still with us, now in close-up [221], watching Mark and Marnie leave the paddock. Back at the luncheon table [222], an amicable chat about Marnie's attitudes toward betting and Mark's family and social position. (The situation is handled through a chain of eighteen shot-reverse portraits rather than from a single camera position, as scripted.) Did she have a tough childhood? – 'I think you did. I think you've had a hard, tough climb.' And then,

'One last inquisitive look' (220-3). Sean Connery in a process shot

'What about *your* tough childhood, Mr Rutland?' 'The old, sad story,' he shrugs, 'promising youth blighted, dragged down by money, position, *noblesse oblige* … Nothing *ever* happens to a family that traditionally marries at least one heiress every other generation.' The race has been running in the background and now, to cap this profoundly revealing little conversation, Mark tells Marnie that her 'wall-eyed reject' won. Marnie believes in horses, 'They're beautiful and … nothing in the world like *people*.' The hunters are always upon her, but Mark inhabits another world – he has been eased into his social position, and speaks with the languid gracility of established wealth, historical continuity, and elevation above bourgeois proprieties. Their class positions being so utterly unmatched – Hitchcock was always precise in his visions of social class – can they possibly meet?

When they have encountered the surveiller one last time and dispensed with him, the confrontation is done. But why does Hitchcock need to have it, why must it take place at a racecourse, and how do the film-maker's actions in shortening, modelling, and tightening the scene bring out concerns vital for the film?

The themes are surveillance, identity, moral culpability, and escape in a (modern, urban) world of detectives and detection (for a fulsome discussion of the relation between surveillance and modernity, see Gunning, 'Tracing'). The self-reflectiveness about cinema and star identity merely nuances an already well-developed thesis centred on the face and its vulnerability to inscription (thus the plethora of close shots and macro-close-ups in the film generally). If Marnie is to be caught out of the blue by someone who knew her in a previous identity, what more likely venue than a large public gathering, such as a sporting event? And what more logical sporting event, given Marnie's general link to horses and the class references in the film, than a race? As a setting, the track takes Marnie's riding and Mark's ownership of horses and expands them into a modern arena where strangers circulate and everyone is seen. Evaluating people and horses at the track is a longstanding social exercise.

Achieved through Hitchcock's modifications is the modelling and modulating of characters, situations, and possibilities, but he was not required by writing deficiencies to make these changes. The script, hardly written off the cuff, emerged after an arduous writing programme involving early work by Joseph Stefano, then a full engagement by Evan Hunter (who, famously, was let off the picture when he refused to write the shipboard honeymoon scene as Hitchcock wanted it), then still another round of labour by newly hired Jay Presson Allen (notable to Hitchcock for her play *The Prime of Miss Jean Brodie*).[55] The track sequence had been sketched, rewritten, entirely reconceived, elaborated, and reshaped in ongoing drafts.

Between the modifications in shooting shown here and those undertaken by George Tomasini in cutting, the effect is to sharpen and clarify the central narrative threads on which Hitchcock wishes to focus. Those repeated dissolves of the strange man as he stares at Marnie and she stares back would have rendered his action of gazing symphonic – a series of Mahlerian breaths in the action – but his importance would then have been magnified as bearer of that dissolving eye. Through repetition, the dissolves would have gained stress visually (just as the name 'Frank Abernathy' does acoustically). Sounding a memory chime is one thing, visually stressing is quite another.

Particularly fascinating is Hitchcock's dissection of a single scripted shot into breakout close-ups that reveal feeling, attitude, and navigational alignment between characters. Given that buried in the racetrack sequence is a fully elaborated but entirely unstated drama of accusation, memory, identification, and probability, we must be enabled to intuit and then follow that 'silent film' while watching the surface story. Hitchcock's camera positions help us know what a character is thinking while looking (and, as Bill Krohn admirably notes, in making this film Hitchcock knew that some thoughts cannot be visualised [*Work*: p. 266]). There are also a number of points where the movement is streamlined: one sees and learns only what is necessary for forward motion. For example, a part of the original [219] showing the jockey bending in his saddle to converse with the trainer is cut. Invoking the trainer would have meant including him in the tale (and hiring an actor), while he has no real place there. Nor, in truth, does the jockey except as a mannequin for displaying that flashy garb (so he is mostly seen in cut-offs that show the silks, not his face).

 Just as the racetrack provided a narratively ideal setting, it was hopeless for live shooting: expensive, hard to light, impossible for sound recording. Shots [192-0], [192] and [215] were made there on 19, 20 and 21 September 1963, along with a large number of backgrounds from, and of, the grandstand and other parts of the track (Robertson to Donnelly, 7 October 1963).[56] Character shots were made on Universal's Stage 31, on 10, 11, 12 and 13 December 1963, for later matte composition. But the blue-screen process failed (and getting the sodium vapour process from Disney, as had been done for *The Birds* [1963], proved impossible), so considerable retakes were made for rear projection. 'We retook I don't know how many feet, hundreds of feet that we shot on *Marnie* on bluescreen. … the blue screen shots all had a blue halo around them, which was the result of the filter being used, and it looked *terrible*' (Robertson in Hall, *Robertson*: pp. 84, 285). However, in the end the effects work is prodigious, well-nigh invisible. To see this sequence is to be at the track, and to deny the critique of Hitchcock's technical infirmities, in a single *coup d'œil*.

5 I Remember Mama

And now to an unravelling.

It is teeming rain as Mark pulls his car up at Bernice's and helps Marnie to the door. She is locked into herself, wet and bedraggled, her long strands of golden hair hanging limp over her shoulders, her eyes red and fixated, her body trembling. Mark apologises that he's sorry to crash in. But all Bernice wants to know is, 'Who are you, Mister? You're not Mr Pendleton!'[57]

As tactfully as possible he explains that he and Marnie are married. She's not well. She hasn't been well for some time. Not, he adds, 'since you had your accident. ... I think you've always called it your "accident".'

Bernice is immediately outraged and on the defensive. Who is this man barging into her house this way? 'You're not married to my Marnie.'

But the time has come, Mark knows, for the truth. All the truth. 'She has no memory of what happened that night. And she *needs* to remember.'

Marnie is sitting at the bottom of the stairs, frozen in another flight. Bernice's chin is raised in disregard. But Mark presses. Does Mrs Edgar know that her beautiful young daughter cannot 'stand to have a man touch her? *Any* man?'

Suddenly, in pathetic fallacy, the thunderstorm fully breaks and Marnie, delivered into a fit, cringes back, tries to enter her own skin. 'Was there a storm that night, Mrs Edgar? Is that why Marnie's so terrified of storms?' The mother lioness guarding the family secret with her life:

BERNICE: Get out of my house! Get out! I don't need any filthy man coming in my house *no more*! You hear me! You get out!

(top) Mark bringing Marnie into her mother's house; (bottom) snarling at Bernice, as he indicates that Marnie cannot be touched by any man

She makes a clumsy move to get at Mark and he must hold her off, but Marnie is staring, 'with widening eyes that suddenly become fixed, dilated'.

Then, from 'Tippi' Hedren – the girl Alfred Hitchcock saw in a Sego commercial on television, the girl who had studied acting with Claudia Franck back in Long Island and then moved with her young daughter to start a career in Los Angeles (Hedren to Franck, 30 August 1962), the girl who on Friday the 13th of October 1961 was telephoned out of the blue and asked to come to Universal and bring 'any photographs or film that I had' (Davis: p. 2), the girl who waited day after day without knowing who wanted to know all about her – 'Monday morning I was asked to go and meet someone else, in the morning, an executive at Universal, and another one and another one and another one. And nobody would tell me the name of the producer' (p. 2) – the girl who was cast and courted and measured and feted, tested and retested and designed for by Edith

'I don't need any filthy man'

Head, photographed all anew (Hedren to Franck, 15 December 1961) and publicised as Hitch's 'new Grace Kelly',[58] the one who made a name for herself in *The Birds* and got the Marnie part over the yearnings of Eva Marie Saint[59] and Walt Disney (who was pushing Susan Hampshire[60]), the one who had stepped into a role so demanding she would appear in 517 of the 528 scenes of the film (Johnson, 'Suspense') – from 'Tippi' Hedren a moment that pushed her to the very heights of what screen acting can be, thanks to but one rather technical performative gesture. She begins to speak in the voice of a five-year-old child. We have had intimation of (preparation for) this before, when in the honeymoon suite her voice broke as she called 'No!' But now the voice is recovered not broken, hailing from the long-lost past – call it a ghost voice, since only in a phantom presence can the little girl who owned it manifest herself:

MARNIE: You let my Mama alone! You hear! You let my Mama alone! You're hurting my Mama!

Mark's head enters the picture. He wants to know, 'Who am I, Marnie?' And for the horrified mother, now seeing her wall of fear starting to collapse, the answer must not be given. 'Shut up, Marnie!' in a sharp bark.

Mark won't have it. 'No, Marnie! … Remember! … *remember*!' A sudden very abrupt inspiration makes him tap the wall three times. She shrinks, mortified. 'What does the tapping mean, Marnie?'

Hitchcock's camera closes in on Marnie's face, using the screen to bound her entirely, so that she has nowhere to go.[61] Trapped in the upcoming memory of her past, she is also trapped in the cinematic frame. And her head has become her fate (see Davenport). We move to Marnie's point of view:

Allen dictated a 'LONG PERSPECTIVE OF A ROOM', set in a slum apartment. 'The perspective is so distorted that it almost seems a great distance away' (scene 506). Hitchcock is converting time into space. 'Its color is washed out almost to grays.' This includes the

costumes and make-up. Slowly 'the perspective lessens and comes NEARER and NEARER to us until the room has attained a normal perspective beyond us'. Normal in perspective, yet it remains a dramaturgically removed space, like the little stage on which, in profound circumstances, players enact a play-within-the-play. Here is a film-within-the-film, set apart, almost floating in the space that Marnie's imagination and memory have opened up in her mother's living room. A slovenly young sailor (Bruce Dern), unshaven, in whites, calls to Young Bernice, somewhere offscreen, 'Hurry up ... get the kid outa the bed.' She emerges, smiling, nuzzling sleepy Little Marnie and settling the girl on the sofa next to the fireplace. But as we get a close-up of Grown Marnie staring out at this, the thunder claps, both here and there, harmonious thunder, thunder across history, and the sailor emerges from the bedroom and approaches the child.

Mark, it is imperative for us to remember, can see none of this. It is Marnie and only Marnie who makes our spectatorial view.

'Who am I, Marnie?'

Mark is there with her *now* but not there with her *then*: two Marks, just as there are two Marnies. And doubled Mark needs to know what is happening as she whimpers:

GROWN MARNIE'S CHILDLIKE VOICE (offscreen): *He* come out ... to me. I don't *like* him ... he smells funny.

SAILOR: Don't cry, little baby ... the Captain's on duty ... all through the night ...

Grown Marnie calls for her Mama now and cries, 'I don't want you. You let me go!'

Is this dream or nightmare? It is dusk, the thunderstorm has erased the day, generating a *Walpurgisnacht* for Marnie. The night operates theatrically, in that the relative brightness of her 'vision' shines out in the surrounding darkness like the blazingly lit stage in a

Hitchcock's conversion of time into space

darkened auditorium (see Schivelbusch, *Night*: p. 206ff.). A dream, a
nightmare, a vision, a memory: they are one and the same, so that all
conceptions of time and measurement, all conceptions of nearness
and distance, are unified.

Young Bernice is now in her slip, furious: 'Get your damn hands
off my kid!' She 'grabs at [the sailor's] hair, aims a hard slap at his
cheek'. He releases Little Marnie and goes at Bernice to defend
himself, all this with the child stunned, 'filming' it frame by frame,
angle by angle (from below), and with Grown Marnie shouting
directions, 'Make him go, Mama!', and Young Bernice 'hitting,
biting, scratching, kicking'. Back and forth from space to space, from
young voice to old.

Bruce Dern and Louise Latham rehearsing the fight sequence

A wonderful Hitchcockian device: Marnie close up, full screen, staring out, with Mark unseen beckoning, 'What is it? What's the matter?' Mark's agony during this sequence has been largely disattended by scholars and critics, even by those who openly profess love for the film. He is experiencing a form of paralysis akin to what besets Jeff Jefferies in *Rear Window* (1954) when through his long-focus lens he sees his beloved Lisa Fremont caught in a murderer's grip and, hobbled in his wheelchair, can do nothing to save her. It is the paralysis of dramatic involvement, when we are enthralled by characters whose fictional gravity we cannot share. Mark Rutland must suddenly know at this moment a horribly theatrical love for Marnie. Like any viewer, he is attached to her characterological, her remote self. Until the horrifying drama resolves, he must stay on the outside.

But Young Bernice and the sailor are entangled – 'My leg … get off …' – and she has collapsed underneath him. 'Mama!' Little Marnie and Grown Marnie are screaming together (Hedren's 'girl'

Two Marnies

voice and her normal voice in a duet). Bernice is in torment. 'You got to help me … I'm hurt, honey …' Writes Allen: 'During these scenes, we have occasionally watched the OLD BERNICE who listens to all this with a frightened tenseness, awed by what she hears.' I think we may take 'awed' with its full religious implication, since Bernice will soon confess she prayed to God that night for Marnie to survive *and forget everything*. To this woman, now, God is speaking through her daughter's retrieval of the past: 'I got to help my Mama!'

The sailor begins to crawl off her mother 'but in doing so he causes her even further pain and she screams'. (A macro-close insert of his hairy leg and her smooth leg intertwined.) Driven, Little Marnie grabs at the poker and lashes out. We hear the meaty sound of the body struck. 'I hit him! I hit him with the stick!' Again, and again. The child's face, 'the widened, shock-blank eyes'. And suddenly:

GROWN MARNIE (child's voice; dreamy, soft, satisfied):   *There*. There now.

But more: As the face of Grown Marnie twists and swells with horror, we see what it is that she sees through Little Marnie's eyes:

THE CAMERA ZOOMS IN until it contains the chest and shoulders of the SAILOR, his white undershirt, whiter now than ever in contrast to the great splashes of red that stain it … the white and red …

Yet this is still insufficient, since it is no objective view of the damaged male body Hitchcock needs us to see Marnie seeing. We must do exactly what the child did, at once shocked and fascinated – there is so much blood. Inward goes the focus, *all the way in*. The blood stain *takes over the screen* (a step far beyond what had been undertaken in *Psycho* [1960] or *The Birds*). The entire rectangle is saturated with red, is converted into blood itself.

And now, the storm eclipsed, Grown Marnie and Little Marnie screaming in unison, the camera eases back to the future, and the past is gone.

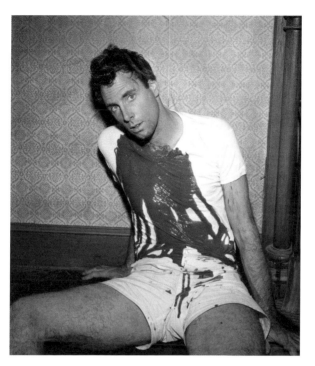

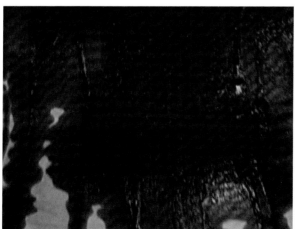

(top) Bruce Dern in costume and make-up test for the bloodied sailor;
(bottom) midway through the focal change, as the sailor's blood takes
over the screen

Marnie and Bernice are jointly released. Bernice has collapsed into her chair, tears on her face, and Marnie is kneeling by her lap, tears upon hers. Only now can Marnie hear how Bernice did love her, how 'You're the only thing I ever did love in this world.' Only now can Bernice recount the story of how a boy named Billy said 'if I'd let him, I could have the sweater. So I let him.'[62] And how she prayed to God that she could keep Marnie. 'It was just I was so young.' Only now can Marnie know that as a child she freed her mother from bondage.

A cadenza before a conclusion:

That bloody screen. It constitutes the human – the living – condition; we all experience everything through blood. Blood is

Production still of Latham and Hedren in the 'release' moment

biology, revivification, identity. It is always somehow blood that speaks, not the calculating mind. Shakespeare knew this, and Hitchcock after him. This is why there is so much apparent debasement, so much reduction, in this film, as, 'nervously loquacious at the edge of an abyss', it drops away from the classed discourse of civility, the tea party of reconciliation, into the unknowable passions of our animal selves. This is why in his film about a girl who must relive the pain she cannot remember, Hitchcock needs a sequence with a fox hunt. This is why his camera intrudes into the honeymoon suite while a man's desire outstrips his breeding. This is why Marnie has a visceral, even erotic relationship with the safe she cracks. This is why splotches of red must be seen garishly, brutally, on – and against – white: Jessie's red gladioli against Marnie's white chrysanthemums, the red macula on the white blouse, the red polka dots on the jockey's white jersey. This is why the knocking becomes a vibration resonating inside Marnie so that she cannot sleep: it is the knock of fate she hears, the knock of life.

Many early respondents to the film misread as a cheap stunt Hitchcock's technique of the red-pulsing screen in Marnie's trauma. William Johnson diagnoses a 'patently blind eye' (p. 40), while *Newsweek* carped, 'When Marnie is upset … Hitchcock put a red filter over the lens, and everything looks red … a device that a Cub Scout with a Brownie would scorn' (Anon, 30 August). Not long afterward, Robin Wood countered with a passionate and intensive discussion of the red suffusions (see *Films*: pp. 175–81). The red suffusions surely offer a truly profound eloquence. What Hitchcock is showing is Grown Marnie's buried remembrance of *the precise vision* she harboured as a little girl, gazing into a dead man's blood and seeing nothing else. It is a primal moment, but also a sincerely aesthetic one; fear but also curiosity. And in seeing it, in seeing that there is *so much* blood,[63] the girl falls into the abysm from which she is only now finding her way back, and up. The critics who think Hitchcock is tricking us are merely afraid to share Marnie's vision.

As to the haunting quality of the remembrance: to establish it through perspectival manipulation, and with aesthetic separation, as Hitchcock has done, to render it upon a stage inside the stage we are watching, is to heighten our own attention, not to Marnie's memory but to the grown Marnie we are watching recapture it. The more charade-like is the play-within-the-play, warns Erving Goffman, the more realistic seem characters caught up watching it (pp. 474–5). Marnie becomes fully realised for us, and gains breath, exactly as the viewer of her own past; and Mark becomes real exactly as the witness to Marnie's witnessing.

They bid Bernice farewell and walk out into the sunny street. The kids are still singing their nursery rhyme, 'Mother, mother, I am ill', but the song doesn't represent Marnie any more. She 'is now aware in a way that she has never known', writes Allen in the 11 February 1964 revisions to the script. 'She is like a person who has been half-blind since birth and who has now been given glasses. She has always been able to see the trees, but now she sees the *leaves*.' Still a little fragile in Mark's hands, Marnie asks him about the future, because '(with solemn decision) I don't want to go to jail. I'd rather stay with you.' Her clear voice, for the first time.

It is Mark who has the curtain line. 'Had you, love?'

Scene 527 shot 17 February 1964: outside Bernice's house in Baltimore. In front from left, Arlene Burns, Judy Erwin, and Libbey Coghlan; at rear from left, Greg Landers, Tim Stafford, and Tony Brown

'Had you', not 'would you'.[64] A delicious subjunctive, which invokes a potent 'if'. If all the past could now disappear … if we could manage to be happy ever after … if he could see what she saw and know the nightmare she knew … if one could only be the person one truly wanted to be. If. They are already in the car, driving off toward that ship at the end of the street (on a new honeymoon?) – 'Away from the street, the children, the past' (scene 528) – down to the end of that blunted forced perspective, right down to the end as far as one can go, then a quick turn and straight on till morning.

Notes

1 After a walk down the hotel corridor, where Alfred Hitchcock performs his cameo by stepping out of a room and briefly looking into the lens.
2 A carry-over from early script drafts by Joseph Stefano and Evan Hunter. Believing that Grace Kelly would play Marnie, Hitchcock planned the shooting to coincide with Rainier and the Princess's annual visit to her parents' home there.
3 Reprising the plunge of Bruno Antony's lighter into a sewer grate in *Strangers on a Train* (1951), which also dealt with neurotic troubles and violent doubles.
4 Hitchcock cast Hartley after seeing her in *Ride the High Country* (Sam Peckinpah, 1962); her comparative youth made her the only member of the supporting cast he needed to meet in person: she showed up wearing glasses, which he said she shouldn't use in the film (Bowser communication).
5 Everett Sloane was originally cast (and was to wear rimless glasses with lenses '*shaped and not flat*' [Robertson to Henshaw]), but retrenched because the part was 'so lamentably small' (Sloane to Hitchcock).
6 'This I say to you with bowed head: there have been some story changes made ... You must be patient with me, ... there is a reason for all of them' (Hitchcock to Graham). 'I'm sorry there have had to be changes, but if a head is bowed I'm glad it's such a distinguished one. In fact, I'm not frightfully fussy about keeping to the letter of a book' (Graham to Hitchcock).
7 With a smile, Hitchcock told Fletcher Markle she rode Forio after each robbery ('Talk with Hitchcock').

8 Contrary to much critical speculation, this rhyme was not inserted as a symbolic gesture by Hitchcock. He asked the children if they knew any skipping rhymes and they immediately came up with the most popular one that year (Smith conversation).
9 *The American Cinematographer Manual* is explicit: 'Traditionally, 1.85 was far and away the most common aspect ratio for motion pictures filmed in the U.S. from the late 1950s until the 1990s' (Hummel: pp. 24–5). Thus, the 1.85 ratio for theatrical projection would likely have been achieved by Burks's compositional reduction of the 1.33 image visible through his viewfinder. Hitchcock knew his film would later be shown on television (in 1.33), and for this a further cropping of the 1.85 would have been necessary (Valentini communication).
10 Sean Connery brought his wife Diane Cilento (1933–2011) to Los Angeles with him. At a BFI Summer School some years later, as Victor Perkins has recounted to me, she was speaking with him about the Baltimore Street set and recalled how everyone had said to Hitchcock, 'Hitch – it's going to look *so* artificial!' He replied, 'Yes, *isn't* it!' (Perkins conversation).
11 For modelling Rutland's, research had been done on the prestigious and very old Philadelphia publisher J. B. Lippincott & Co. (founded 1836).
12 Seeing a rough cut, Jay Presson Allen recommended eliminating the kiss, 'although I think it would be useful in the trailer'. Hitchcock refused ('Comments on Screening').
13 Writing of the mirror as seen by Walter Benjamin, Tom Gunning notes

that it 'relies not only on separation and insulation but also on disguise and illusion, as the optics of interior space take on the complexity of the phantasmagoria' ('*Intérieur*': pp. 106–7). The illusion of Marnie in the mirror is utterly phantasmagorical.

14 After directions were given to retake this insert, shooting down to 'see the bottle of ink spill onto the sleeve' (Robertson to Green, 18 December), the decision was made to have Hedren 'dip her pen into the red ink'; then 'a small drop of red ink, not more than 1/8" in diameter, will drop on her sleeve' (Robertson to Green, 27 December).

15 Sean Connery was cast as a result of Hitchcock and Jay Presson Allen watching him in a James Bond film. When he came onscreen they turned to one another and said, 'That's him' (Allen conversation). He found himself 'interested in seeing Hitch work, as well as in doing everything I could to make it easy for him' (Connery in Chandler, pp. 272–3). So warmly was he received among the cast and crew that they presented him with an engraved wristwatch when shooting wrapped. Norman Lloyd recollected to me, 'He took off his own watch and threw it away' (Lloyd conversation).

16 In Hitchcock's next film, *Torn Curtain* (1966), Professor Lindt will 'skip steps' in the same way.

17 Only the exterior approach was shot on location at Howard Johnson's, Highway 1, junction 320, Wayne, Pennsylvania. The rest was filmed on Stage 21 at Universal on 27 and 30 December 1963, with decorations and accoutrements sent to the studio by Howard Johnson's head office (McLaughlin to Brown), and using rear projection.

18 Jay Presson Allen wanted to see more of Cousin Bob in the film; Hitchcock did not ('Comments on Screening').

19 A knowing nod on Allen's part to Amanda Wingfield in Tennessee Williams's *The Glass Menagerie* (1944).

20 Montage sequences were popular in 1960s Hollywood.

21 Supplied by Sulka and Co. of Park Avenue (Sulka memo). Six robes were shipped to Hitchcock for selection, on 7 November 1963.

22 And Mrs Danvers brushed her mistress's in *Rebecca* (1940).

23 'MARNIE'S "No" when MARK strips her clothes off should be looped with a real scream' (Allen, 'Comments on Screening').

24 The novel neutralises the event: 'My frock slipped down. I felt an awful feeling of something that seemed to be half embarrassment and half disgust' (Graham: p. 172).

25 The pose is borrowed from Gustav Klimt's 'The Kiss' (1908–9).

26 Casting director Robert Bowser confirmed to me that the word 'rape' was never used.

27 On the *acousmêtre* in general, see Michel Chion, who writes: 'Acousmatic, specifies an old dictionary, "is said of a sound that is heard without its cause or source being seen."' Chion notes that when we cannot directly connect the acousmatic presence to someone, 'we get a special being, a kind of talking and acting shadow' (pp. 18, 21).

28 Graham's novel includes two detailed reports of early thieving: one during Marnie's childhood, filmed on 4 March 1964, with Melody Thomas as the young Marnie, and Sally Smith, Robin Adair, and Susan Cupito as her friends – this sequence was cut in the final edit; and one while she works at a movie theatre, which was planned for 12 March but, owing to a gelid détente between Hitchcock and Hedren at this point, not filmed (Bowser communication). Marnie was to have craftily caused Coca-Cola to drip onto customers from the balcony, distracting the manager; also included was a brief moment with the projectionist, ranting about the faulty lens and how it distorted the projection of credits.

29 In the specific sense of a chiaroscuro underpainting, made famous by Raphael (1483–1520) (Personal conversation).

30 Letting drop an earlier thought that it 'might be good to take some license and put the sound of the sea going by' ('Dubbing Notes': p. 4).

31 Charles Barr suggests the use of dogs as 'moral touchstones' at least in Hitchcock's British work (p. 189). On Bernice Edgar's picture, see Pomerance, 'Dogs': pp. 59–60, where I note the 'motherliness' inherent in the doggy poses and the benignity with which these dogs 'overlook the proceedings' we see in the house. The Landseer is clearly visible in the lower photograph on p. 21 here.

32 Connery 'was playing a Philadelphian … he had to get rid of the Scottish brogue', Hitchcock's assistant Peggy Robertson remembered. 'So we ordered up a lot of records … lots of different things with people speaking in Philadelphia accents … [Sean] said to me, "What are all these records doing here?" And I said, "Well, they're for you to study the Philadelphia accent." So he said, "I don't want to study the Philadelphia accent. And what's more, I'm not going to!" … So he played the whole picture with a Scottish brogue' (Hall, *Robertson*: p. 95).

33 Diegetically speaking, near the Red Fox Inn, Middleburg, Virginia, for permission to use the name and image of which Hitchcock's staff made request (Brown to Grasty).

34 Louise Latham, a Texan then resident in New York, had been proposed by Jay Presson Allen. Hitchcock screened 'The Hour before Doomsday' from *The Defenders* as an audition (Unsigned Note).

35 For the rear view and fields behind Wykwyn, the production used William B. Willson's Wyllpen Farm, West Chester, Pennsylvania ('Locations and Contacts').

36 Susan Cocks of Hermitage Farm, Unionville, was slated to stand in for Hedren in the group riding scenes; a Miss Boyce for Diane Baker.

37 Background plates of the hunt sequence had been planned during an actual hunt scheduled for 22 November 1963. Because of the assassination of John F. Kennedy, the event was cancelled and shot instead on Tuesday 26 November, from 11:00 a.m. until 3:30 p.m., with sixty riders and forty-two hounds. This was also the first day of studio filming, postponed from the day before, which was overshadowed by the presidential funeral. Lew Wasserman had ordered that work continue, as 'the president would expect' (Coleman: p. 321).

38 This moment strikingly resembles one in Roberto Rossellini's

Stromboli (1950) when Karen (Ingrid Bergman), trapped in a painful marriage on a desolate isle and trying to befriend her husband by visiting him when he is fishing with the other villagers, suddenly sees a school of tuna swimming with frenzy in the net and then, one fish in particular speared and hauled out of the sea. She is this creature at this moment, much as Marnie is the cornered fox.

39 The word 'Shermanising' refers to the brutal, 'scorched earth' tactics of General William Tecumseh Sherman (1820–91), who led Union forces against the Confederacy and notably captured Atlanta for the North.

40 Devised at Paramount by Farciot Edouart in 1938 and borrowed for some shots here.

41 The kill shot is a process composite with Forio in rear projection.
His whimpering can be brought to a sudden halt because it is on tape; his arrestment of movement would have been a behaviour learned from his wrangler, the actor Jack Carry, whose off-camera stimulations produced the twitches (Conversation with Cox). (See also Moral: p. 117).

42 'Starting in the morning of the Hunt Sequence, start eye make-up to show distress, increase tragedy in the eyes from the Hunt until the finish of the picture. … Test red or pink rim on the inner rim of the eye,' Hitchcock had suggested (Brown and Green).

43 Hedren's career as a model had prepared her. 'I had had so much experience doing commercials, which is extremely technical. I mean you're not acting, you are specifically working with a product, working with an object, and it's all very technical. I was used to the camera and the lights, so that didn't bother me at all' (Davis: pp. 4, 6).

44 Off Placerita Canyon Road near Santa Clarita, California, with Betsy Irvine doubling for Hedren.

45 Diane Baker had projected herself into Marnie's character for a moment, as she recollected to Charlotte Chandler. 'I was terribly nervous for the tea-pouring scene. I was afraid my hand would shake and the tea cup would rattle in the saucer or that I would spill the tea pouring it' (p. 278). Baker does not touch the teapot or a teacup in the scene.

46 In producing 'droppage and spillage', a strange echo of Bernice's fear that the flowers Marnie replaces might produce 'dripping'.

47 Allen had suggested cutting this line, but Hitchcock wished to keep it ('Comments on Screening'). I suggest in *An Eye for Hitchcock* that in changing Emerson's 'the youth' to 'then youth', Mark replaces a dramatic description with a 'moral prescription apposite to [Lil's] particular circumstance at this moment' (pp. 161–2).

48 Numbers in square brackets [192] are from Allen's script; numbers with hyphenated suffixes [192-0] are Hitchcock's additions with my numberings.

49 Behind and in rear projection, as are almost all the racing fans shown in this sequence.

50 Why, indeed, see him rolling the paper at all? Recollect Hitchcock's lesson to Allen about screenwriting, quoted here in Chapter 2 (p. 23).

51 'There are so many wonderful things to tell you and it's impossible in a letter.

But, I will say he tested me in every way he could think of, and I loved every second of it' (Hedren to Franck, 29 November 1961).

52 And Hitchcock had a heartfelt preference for looking up. As he told Alexander Golitzen when they worked on *Foreign Correspondent* (1940) together, 'The best way to see anything is in low camera setups' (Hall, *Golitzen*: p. 54).

53 Borrowed directly from the classical George Herbert Mead (pp. 173–8).

54 This effect is accomplished in the laboratory, where the red values of an image can be heightened to order.

55 Paid $26,500 for her involvement, Allen was to work 'with Mr Hitchcock, directly from the book itself. She will not read any of the MARNIE material which was written by Joe Stefano or Evan Hunter' (Unsigned to Robertson; Robertson to Writers Guild).

56 Colour slides of various uniforms and crowds were made on 18 October (Robertson to Donnelly, 21 October 1963). The voice of race announcer Morris Tobe was recorded for script use as he calls Telepathy's race (Unsigned Memo). It was the actor Stuart Margolin who recorded the sound (Bowser communication).

57 Bernice is aptly mis-remembering the fictitious boss Mr Pemberton's name. Asking 'Who is Mr Pendleton?', Mark is making a double joke.

58 'She preserves the image of the classic "fine" blonde beauty reminiscent of Princess Grace' (*Women's Wear Daily*).

'Much of "Tippi's" attraction for [Hitchcock] stems from her resemblance to his former pet, Grace Kelly' (Abramson). See also Hamilton.

59 'When I told Eva that you were going to do the film version of 'MARNIE', she begged me to get in touch with you and let you know how much she loved the book and how wonderful it would be for her to work with you again and to do the film. … As far as Eva is concerned, should you want her for the picture, she would be a very happy girl' (Hirshan to Hitchcock).

60 'I am quite enthusiastic about this young lady and happy to call her to your attention. … If you are contemplating doing "Marnie", you might want to consider Susan' (Disney to Hitchcock). Hampshire had begged Disney from London to write to Hitchcock.

61 I once heard Edward T. Hall tell about a schizophrenic girl whose self-portraits all looked like this. One day he was inspired to lead her into a field, where she suddenly sighed with relief: 'Oh! I can breathe!'

62 On 10 June 1964 this line was almost cut, at Hitchcock's suggestion. Three hundred and fifty prints had already been released, fifty-five of them abroad, and the film was due to open in England on 9 July. In the final cut, the dialogue is untouched.

63 'Yet who would have thought the old man/to have had so much blood in him' (*Macbeth* V.i.2163–4).

64 In an overdub.

Credits

Marnie
USA/1964

Directed by
Alfred Hitchcock
Produced by
Geoffrey Stanley Inc.
Screenplay by
Jay Presson Allen
From the novel by
Winston Graham
Director of Photography
Robert Burks, A.S.C.
Film Editor
George Tomasini, A.C.E.
Production Designer
Robert Boyle
Music Composed by
Bernard Herrmann

© 1964. Universal
Pictures Co.
Production Companies
Universal Pictures
Co./Geoffrey Stanley Inc.

Location Manager
Pierre 'Frenchie' Valin
1st Assistant Directors
James H. Brown
Hilton A. Green
2nd Assistant Director
Pat Casey
**Assistant to Mr
Hitchcock**
Peggy Robertson
**Mr Hitchcock's
Secretary**
Sue Gauthier
Assistant Art Director
Bob Luthardt

Matte Artist
Al Whitlock
Sketch Artist
Harold Michelson
Set Designs
Jim Bachman
Angelo Graham
Ed Elliot
Ernie Jaeger
Set Decorator
George Milo
Script Supervisor
Lois Thurman
Assistant Film Editor
Bud Hoffman
Editorial Assistant
Gilbert Hudson
Camera Operator
Leonard South
**1st Assistant
Cameraman**
Eugene Liggett
**2nd Assistant
Cameraman**
John W. Hussey
Still Photographer
Rollie Lane
**Special Still
Photographs**
Robert Willoughby
Gaffer
Babe Stafford
Best Boy
George Dahlquist
Electricians
Paul Jacobsen
Robert Kaine
Glenn Knight
A. G. Sandsberry
Lew Williman

Key Grip
Dean Paup
2nd Grip
George Hudder
Grips
C. E. Flesher
R. L. Sordal
Special Effects
Walter Hammond
Property Master
Tony Lombardo
Assistant Prop Man
Robert Rentch
Props
Perry Gabbard
Sound Mixer
William Russell
Sound Recording
James V. Swartz
Boom Man
John Erlinger
Cableman
Victor Goode
**Miss Hedren's and Miss
Baker's Costumes**
Edith Head
Hats by
Rex
Costume Supervisor
Vincent Dee
Women's Costumes
Rita Riggs
Men's Costumes
James Linn
Make-up Artists
Jack Barron
Robert Dawn
Howard Smit, S.M.A.
Body Make-up, Women
Edith Smit

Miss Hedren's Hairstyles Created by
Alexandre of Paris
Hairstylist
Virginia Darcy, C.H.S.
Wava Green
Craft Serviceman
Walter Pelican
Driver
Barney Bradshaw
Standby Painter
Arthur Davis
Production Secretary
Pat Perry
Casting
Jere Henshaw
Robert Bowser
Extra Casting
Karl Brindle
Budget
John Oser
Publicity
David Golding
Unit Publicist
Harold Mendelsohn
Legal
James Weinberg
Music Editing
Dick Harris
Donald K. Harris

Second Unit:
Director
William Witney
Assistant Director
James H. Brown
Cameraman
Rex Wimpy
Camera Assistant
James R. Connell

Camera Operator
William J. Dodds
Key Grip
Ken Smith
Matte Artist
Al Whitlock
Propman
R. Dudley 'Ace' Holmes
Accountant
Donald H. Wyman

CAST:
'Tippi' Hedren
Marnie Edgar
Sean Connery
Mark Rutland
Diane Baker
Lil Mainwaring
Louise Latham
Bernice Edgar
Alan Napier
Mr Rutland
Bob Sweeney
Cousin Bob
Martin Gabel
Sidney Strutt
S. John Launer
Sam Ward
Mariette Hartley
Susan Clabon
Linden Chiles
Artie Nelson
Milton Selzer
man at racetrack
Bruce Dern
sailor
Henry Beckman
Barnaby Hale
detectives
Meg Wyllie
Mrs Turpin (farmer's wife)

Anne Loos
Miss Blakely
Edith Evanson
Rita – office cleaner
Rupert Crosse
nightwatchman
Hilda Plowright
maid at Wykwyn
John Alvin
Ralph (driver at the Red Fox Inn)
Lillian Bronson
Mrs Maitland
Irene Martin
Howard Johnson's waitress
Paulle Clark
Howard Johnson's cashier
John Hart
Reverend Gillian
Louise Lorimer
Mrs Strutt
Carmen Phillips
Miss Croft (Strutt's secretary)
Kimberly Beck
Jessie Cotton
Claire Wilcox
Little Marnie
Tony Brown
Arlene Burns
Libbey Coghlan
Judy Erwin
Debora Bowser
Greg Landers
Tim Stafford
children on street
Hal Gould
Mr Garrod
Thomas McBride
taxi driver

Sarah Collingwood
Alice Dudley
Pearl Shear
Barbara Slate
secretaries
Barbara Babcock
Ruth Clifford
Tom Curtis
Alex Finlayson
Stephen Mines
Molly Roden
party guests
Charles P. Thompson
Charlie (elderly
gentleman at party)
Kendrick Huxham
butler at Wykwyn
Bryan O'Byrne
manservant at Wykwyn
**Mr Stewart's Cheshire
Hounds, Unionville,
Pennsylvania**
the fox hunt
Bob Lyons
master of the hunt

May Boss
Jean Eppers
John Eppers
Stephanie Eppers
Lenny Geer
Donna Hall
Edith Happy
Mel Harris
Robert Hoy
Alan Pinson
Mary Statler
riders at the hunt
Gene Hunter Foley
Greg Rhinelander
Edwin Stanbridge
bits
May Boss
Jimmie Booth
stunts
Carol Sloan
Ramon Martinez
stand-ins

Miss Boyce
Susan Cocks
Donna Hall
Betsy Irvine
Missie O'Brien
Kay Tester
doubles for Marnie
Stuart Margolin
voice of Atlantic City
racecourse announcer

Release details:
UK theatrical release on
9 July 1964. US theatrical
release by Universal
Pictures on 22 July 1964.
Running time:
130 minutes

Bibliography

Books and articles

Abramson, Martin. 'What Hitchcock Does with His Blood Money', *Cosmopolitan* (January 1964).

Allen, Richard. 'An Interview with Jay Presson Allen', *The Hitchcock Annual 2000–1*, vol. 9, pp. 3–22.

Anon. 'Review of *Marnie*', *Newsweek* (30 August 1964).

——. 'Review of *Marnie*', *Saturday Review* (5 September 1964).

Archer, Eugene. 'Hitchcock's "Marnie", with Tippi Hedren and Sean Connery', *New York Times* (23 July 1964). Available online at: <partners.nytimes.com/library/film/072364hitch-marnie-review.html>. Accessed 11 July 2013.

Ardrey, Robert. *African Genesis: A Personal Investigation into the Animal Origins and Nature of Man* (New York: Dell, 1969).

Auiler, Dan. *Hitchcock's Notebooks* (New York: Avon, 1999).

Barr, Charles. *English Hitchcock* (Moffat: Cameron & Hollis, 1999).

Bellour, Raymond. 'Hitchcock, The Enunciator', *Camera Obscura* 2 (1977), pp. 67–92.

Chandler, Charlotte. *It's Only a Movie: Alfred Hitchcock, a Personal Biography* (New York: Simon & Schuster, 2005).

Chion, Michel. *The Voice in Cinema*, trans. Claudia Gorbman (New York: Columbia University Press, 1999).

Claiborne, Craig. *Craig Claiborne's Southern Cooking* (New York: New York Times Books, 1985).

——. *Craig Claiborne's The New York Times Food Encyclopedia* (New York: New York Times Books, 1987).

Coleman, Herbert. *The Hollywood I Knew: A Memoir: 1916–1988* (Lanham, MD: Scarecrow Press, 2003).

Connolly, Mike. Comments on *Marnie* in *The Hollywood Reporter* (12 December 1963).

Davenport, Guy. *Objects on a Table: Harmonious Disarray in Art and Literature* (Washington DC: Counterpoint, 1998).

Davis, Ronald L. *Interview with Tippi Hedren*, no. 257. Ronald L. Davis Oral History Collection, DeGolyer Library, Southern Methodist University, 24 July 1982, HER.

Deleuze, Gilles. *Cinema 2: The Time-Image*, trans. Hugh Tomlinson and Robert Galeta (Minneapolis: University of Minnesota Press, 1989).

Freud, Sigmund. 'The Relation of the Poet to Day-dreaming', in *On Creativity and the Unconscious: Papers on the Psychology of Art, Literature, Love, Religion*, selected by Benjamin Nelson (New York: Harper & Row, 1958), pp. 44–54.

Goffman, Erving. *Frame Analysis: An Essay on the Organization of Experience* (Cambridge, MA: Harvard University Press, 1974).

Graham, Winston. *Marnie* (London: Pan, 2013).

Gunning, Tom. 'Tracing the Individual Body: Photography, Detectives, and Early Cinema', in Leo Charney and Vanessa R. Schwartz (eds), *Cinema and the Invention of Modern Life* (Berkeley: University of California Press, 1995), pp. 15–45.

——. 'The Exterior as *Intérieur*: Benjamin's Optical Detective', *boundary 2* vol. 30 no. 1 (Spring 2003), pp. 105–30.

Hall, Barbara. *Oral History with Alexander Golitzen* (Beverly Hills, CA: Academy of Motion Picture Arts and Sciences, 1992).

——. *Oral History with Peggy Robertson* (Beverly Hills, CA: Academy of Motion Picture Arts and Sciences, 2002).

Hamilton, Jack. 'Hitchcock's New Grace Kelly: Tippi Hedren', *Look* (4 December 1962), pp. 53–8.

Hitchcock, Alfred. 'Core of the Movie – The Chase', in Sydney Gottlieb (ed.), *Hitchcock on Hitchcock: Selected Writings and Interviews* (Berkeley: University of California Press, 1995), pp. 125–32.

Hummel, Rob. *American Cinematographer Manual*, 8th edn (Hollywood, CA: ASC Press, 2001).

Hunter, Evan. *Me and Hitch* (London: Faber and Faber, 1977).

Innis, Harold Adams. *The Bias of Communication* (Toronto: University of Toronto Press, 1968).

Johnson, Erskine. 'This Suspense Is His Own', *Akron Beacon-Journal* (13 January 1964). Edith Head Papers, Margaret Herrick Library, Academy of Motion Picture Arts and Sciences, Beverly Hills, California.

Johnson, William. 'Review of *Marnie*', *Film Quarterly* vol. 18 no. 1 (Autumn 1964), pp. 38–42.

Krohn, Bill. 'They Made *The Birds*: Round Table with Hitchcock's Designers Albert Whitlock, Robert Boyle, Harold Michelson, Richard Edlund', *Cahiers du cinéma* vol. 337 (June 1982), pp. 36–48. The English version quoted here is from the original tape transcription, courtesy Bill Krohn.

——. *Hitchcock at Work* (London: Phaidon, 2000).

McElhaney, Joe. *The Death of Classical Cinema: Hitchcock, Lang, Minnelli* (Albany: State University of New York Press, 2006).

McIntosh, Mary. 'Changes in the Organization of Thieving', in Stanley Cohen (ed.), *Images of Deviance* (Harmondsworth, Middlesex: Penguin, 1973), pp. 98–133.

McLuhan, Marshall. *Understanding Media: The Extensions of Man* (New York: McGraw-Hill, 1964).

Markle, Fletcher. 'A Talk with Hitchcock', originally aired on CBC *Telescope*, 1964.

Mead, George Herbert. *Mind, Self, and Society: From the Standpoint of a Social Behaviorist* (Chicago: University of Chicago Press, 1934).

Moral, Tony Lee. *Hitchcock and the Making of Marnie* (Lanham, MD: Scarecrow Press, 2002).

Mulvey, Laura. *Visual and Other Pleasures* (Bloomington: Indiana University Press, 1989).

Perkins, V. F. *Film as Film: Understanding and Judging Movies* (Harmondsworth, Middlesex: Penguin, 1972).

Pomerance, Murray. *An Eye for Hitchcock* (New Brunswick, NJ: Rutgers University Press, 2004).

——. *The Eyes Have It: Cinema and the Reality Effect* (New Brunswick, NJ: Rutgers University Press, 2013).

——. 'Hitchcock Goes to the Dogs', *Film International* vol. 11 nos. 3–4 (2013), pp. 49–63.

Rothman, William. *Hitchcock – The Murderous Gaze*, 2nd edn (Albany: State University of New York Press, 2012).

Scheff, Thomas J. 'Audience Awareness and Catharsis in Drama', *The Psychoanalytic Review* vol. 63 no. 4 (Winter 1976–7), pp. 529–54.

Schivelbusch, Wolfgang. *Disenchanted Night: The Industrialization of Light in the Nineteenth Century*, trans. Angela Davies (Berkeley: University of California Press, 1995).

——. *The Culture of Defeat: On National Trauma, Mourning, and Recovery*, trans. Jefferson Chase(New York: Henry Holt, 2001).

Scott, Marvin B. and Stanford M. Lyman. 'Accounts', *American Sociological Review* vol. 33 no. 1 (February 1968), pp. 46–62.

Spoto, Donald. *The Dark Side of Genius: The Life of Alfred Hitchcock* (New York: Ballantine, 1984).

Thomas, Deborah. 'Self-Possession and Dispossession in *Marnie*', *The Hitchcock Annual*, vol. 15 (2006–7), pp. 107–21.

Truffaut, François. *Hitchcock*, trans. Helen Scott (New York: Touchstone, 1985).

Wharton, Flavia. 'Review of *Marnie*', *Films in Review* vol. 15 no. 7 (August–September 1964), pp. 436–8.

Wood, Robin. 'Looking at *The Birds* and *Marnie* through the *Rear Window*', *Cineaction* vol. 50 (September 1999), pp. 80–5.

——. *Hitchcock's Films Revisited*, rev. edn (New York: Columbia University Press, 2002).

Žižek, Slavoj. 'The Hitchcockian Blot', in *Looking Awry: An Introduction to Jacques Lacan through Popular Culture* (Cambridge, MA: MIT Press, 1992), pp. 88–106.

Archival materials

HER = Margaret Herrick Library of the Academy of Motion Picture Arts and Sciences, Beverly Hills, California.

Allen, Jay Presson. 'Comments on *Marnie* Screening', 24 March 1964, Alfred Hitchcock Collection, HER.

——. Personal conversation, November 2003.

Bowser, Robert. Personal communication, 19 October 2013.

Brown, James. Letter to William Grasty, Red Fox Inn, re. permission to use name and image, 8 November 1963, *Marnie* clearances file 441, Alfred Hitchcock Collection, HER.

Brown, James and Hilton Green. 'Notes from Make-up Meeting with Mr Hitchcock', 8 November 1963, *Marnie* make-up file 467, Alfred Hitchcock Collection, HER.

Burks, Robert. Note to Jack Bishop, Paramount Pictures, re. diminishing lens, 12 March 1964, file 435, Robert Boyle Collection, HER.

Conversation with Monty Cox, 25 August 2013.

Disney, Walt. Letter to Alfred Hitchcock, regarding Susan Hampshire, 4 December 1962, *Marnie* casting file 440, Alfred Hitchcock Collection, HER.

Dubbing Notes from Alfred Hitchcock for *Marnie*, *Marnie* dubbing file 449, Alfred Hitchcock Collection, HER.

Graham, Winston. Letter to Alfred Hitchcock, re. changes in the book, 18 December 1963, Winston Graham file, Alfred Hitchcock Collection, HER.

Haines, Richard W. Personal communication, 26 August 2013.

Hedren, Tippi. Letter to Claudia Franck, re. move to Los Angeles, 30 August 1961, Claudia Franck Papers, HER.

——. Letter to Claudia Franck, re. working with Hitchcock, 29 November 1961, Claudia Franck Papers, HER.

——. Letter to Claudia Franck, re. control of her publicity, 15 December 1961, Claudia Franck Papers, HER.

Hirshan, Leonard. Letter to Alfred Hitchcock, re. Eva Marie Saint, 28 November 1962, Marnie casting file 440, Alfred Hitchcock Collection, HER.

Hitchcock, Alfred. Letter to Winston Graham, re. changes in the book, 10 December 1963, Winston Graham file, Albert Hitchcock Collection, HER.

——. Transcript of Discussion Between Alfred Hitchcock, Bob Boyle, and Evan Hunter, 4 February 1963, Marnie story outline (production design) file 490, Alfred Hitchcock Collection, HER.

Krohn, Bill. Personal conversation, 15 July 2013.

Lloyd, Norman. Personal conversation, 17 July 2013.

'Locations and Contacts' memorandum, Marnie Second Unit file 487, Alfred Hitchcock Collection, HER.

McLaughlin, George T. Letter to James Brown, re. Howard Johnson's items, 4 December 1963, Marnie clearances file 441, Alfred Hitchcock Collection, HER.

Memorandum from A. Sulka and Co., Park Avenue, re. robe shipment, Marnie wardrobe file 500, Alfred Hitchcock Collection, HER.

Perkins, Victor. Personal conversation, 20 April 2014.

Robertson, Peggy. Letter to Writers Guild of America, re. Jay Presson Allen, 4 June 1963, Jay Presson Allen file, Alfred Hitchcock Collection, HER.

——. Inter-Office Communication to Paul Donnelly, re. staff gratuity, 7 October 1963, Marnie accounting file 428, Alfred Hitchcock Collection, HER.

——. Inter-Office Communication to James Brown, re. location trip research, 18 October 1963, Alfred Hitchcock Collection, HER.

——. Inter-Office Communication to Paul Donnelly, re. colour slides of Atlantic City racecourse, 21 October 1963, Marnie accounting file 428, Alfred Hitchcock Collection, HER.

——. Inter-Office Communication to Bob Boyle, re. Ward's office, 24 October 1963, Marnie studio file 492, Alfred Hitchcock Collection, HER.

——. Inter-Office Communication to Jere Henshaw, re. Everett Sloane's glasses, 31 October 1963, Marnie casting file 440, Alfred Hitchcock Collection, HER.

——. Inter-Office Communication to Paul Donnelly, re. toupees for Sean Connery, 29 November 1963, Marnie accounting file 428, Alfred Hitchcock Collection, HER.

——. Inter-Office Communication to Hilton Green, re. retaking of scene 131 with blood on sleeve, 18 December 1963, *Marnie* production file 473, Alfred Hitchcock Collection, HER.

——. Inter-Office Communication to Hilton Green, re. retaking of scene 131 with blood on sleeve, 27 December 1963, *Marnie* production file 473, Alfred Hitchcock Collection, HER.

——. Letter to Sean Connery, re. shooting completion, 20 March 1964, *Marnie* Sean Connery file 442, Alfred Hitchcock Collection, HER.

Shurlock, Geoffrey. Letter to Peggy Robertson, re. problems, 7 October 1963, *Marnie*-MPAA file 468, Alfred Hitchcock Collection, HER.

Sloane, Everett. Letter to Alfred Hitchcock, re. withdrawal from *Marnie*, 17 November 1963, *Marnie* casting file 440, Alfred Hitchcock Collection, HER.

Smith, Debora. Personal conversation, 7 October 2013.

Unsigned Memorandum to Peggy Robertson, re. Jay Presson Allen salary, 3 June 1963, Jay Presson Allen file, Alfred Hitchcock Collection, HER.

Unsigned Note, re. Jay Presson Allen and Louise Latham, 9 December 1963, file 435, Robert Boyle Collection, HER.

Unsigned Memorandum, re. contacts for Morris Tobe, undated, Robert Boyle file 435, Alfred Hitchcock Collection, HER.

Valentini, Sean. Personal communication, 26 August 2013.